CAR WASH ART

Inspiration for the Book
and
Artistic Advisor

Jennifer Sobreiro

Photos By

D. Santora

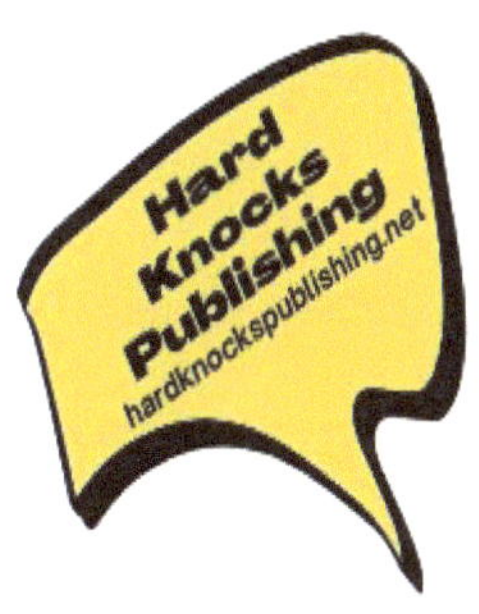

hardknockspublishing.net

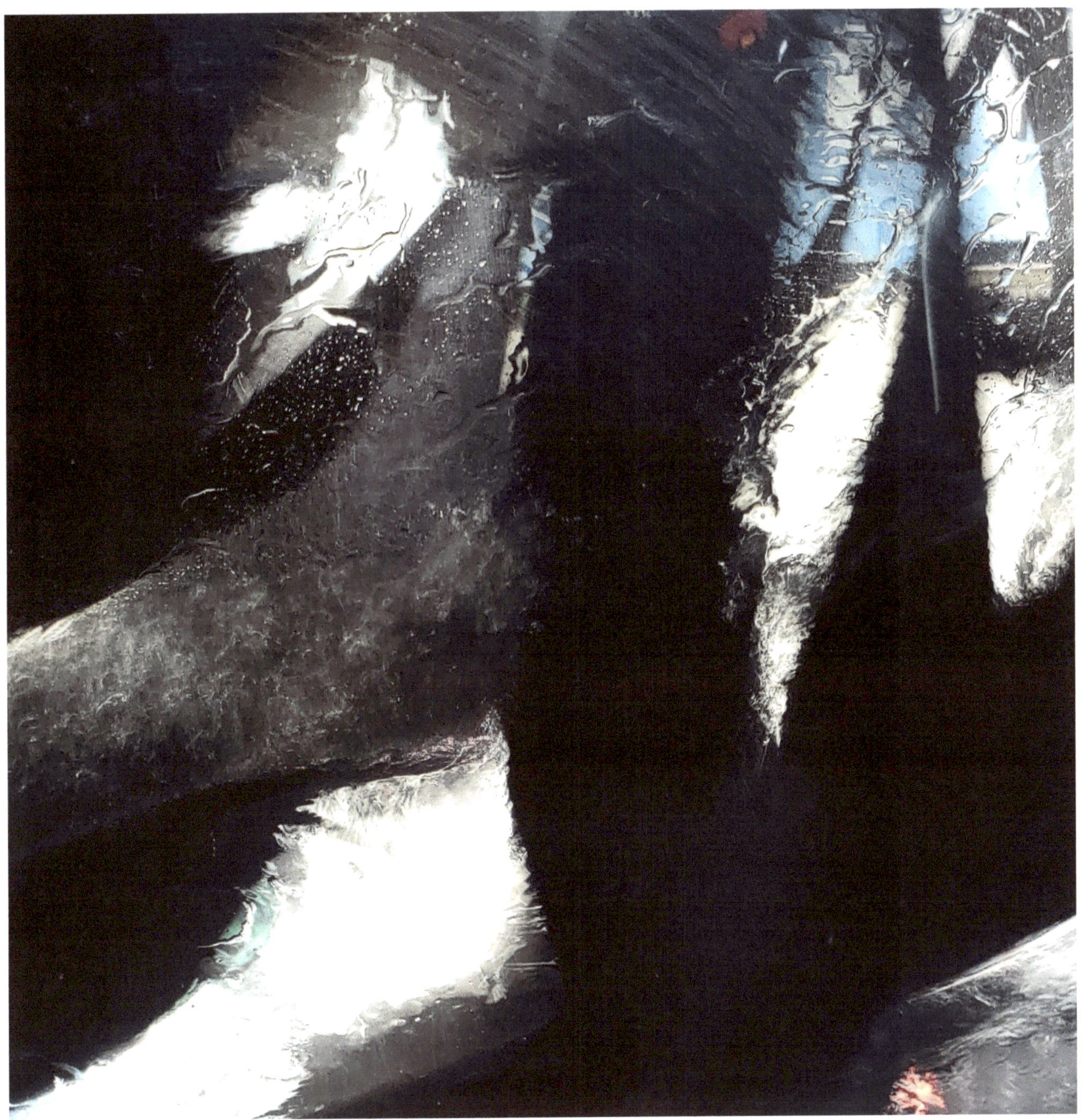

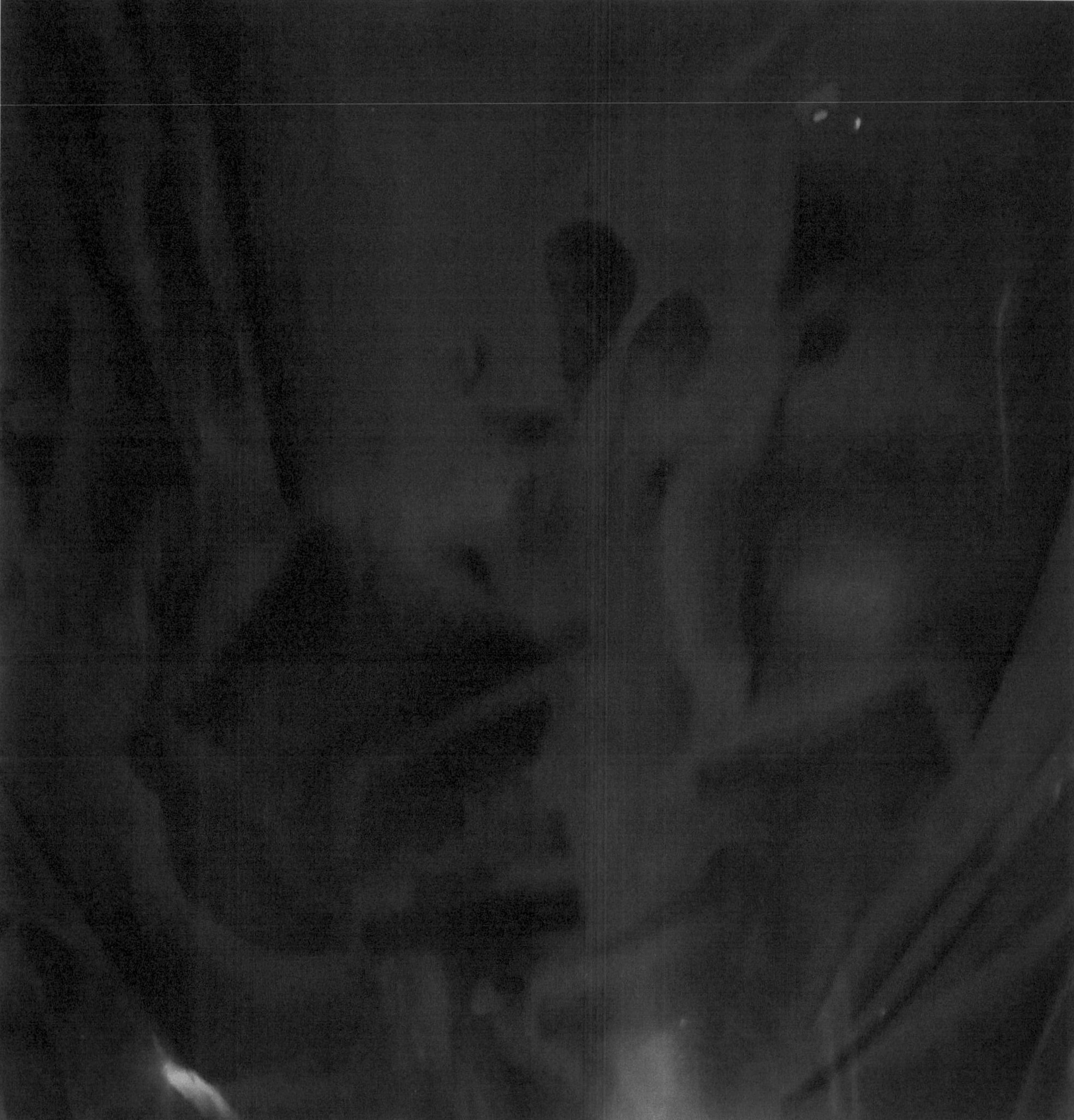

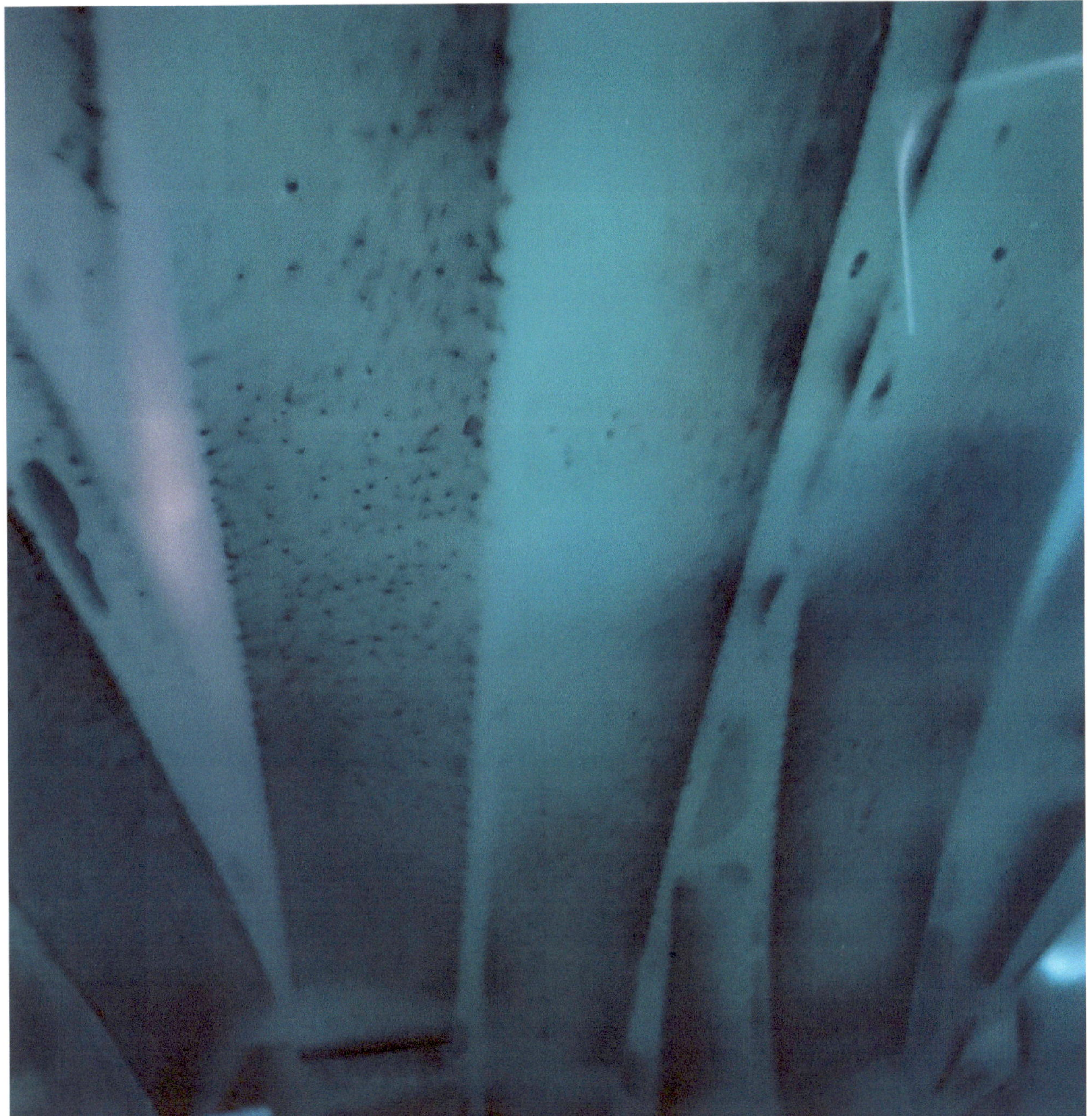

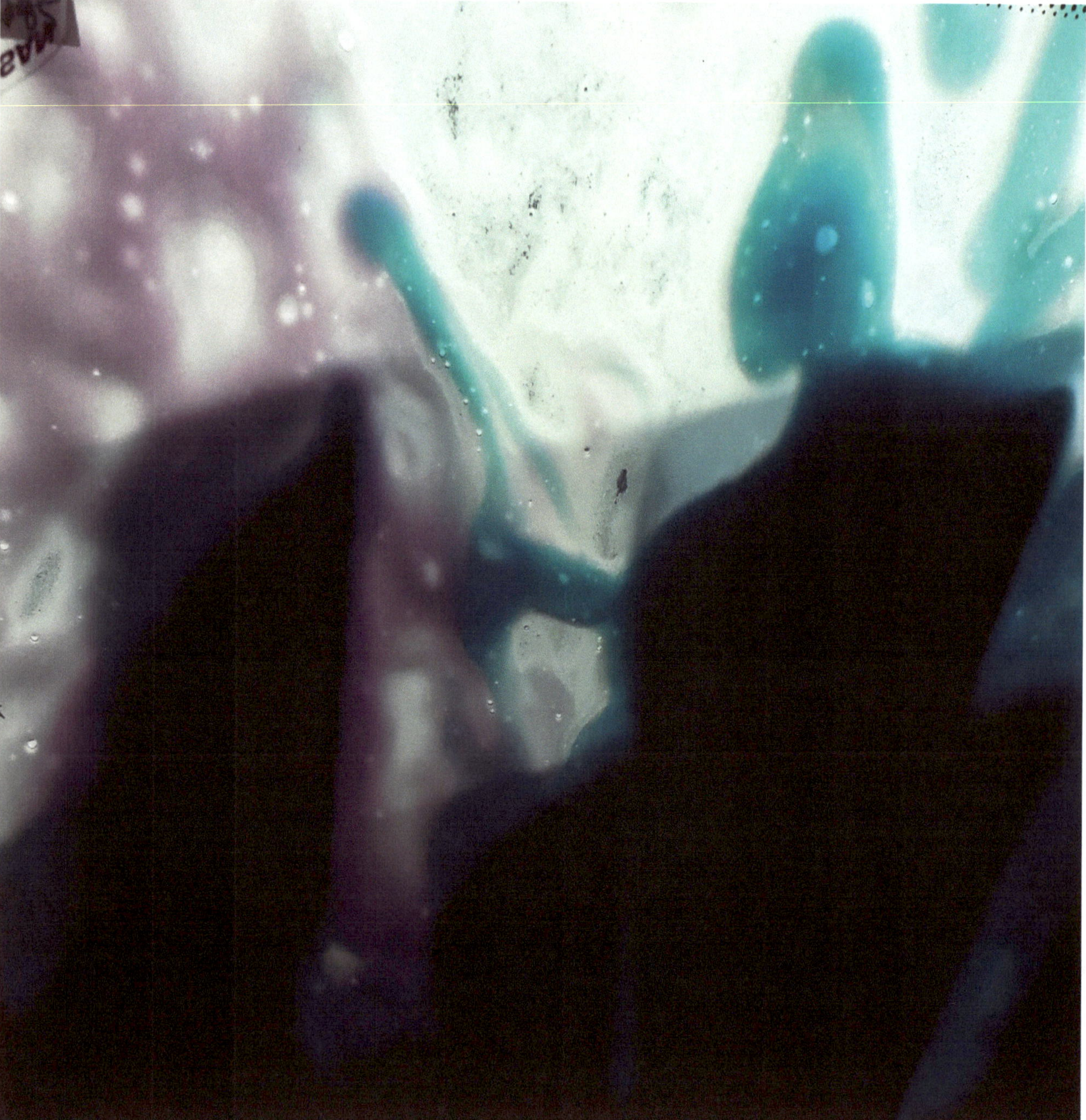

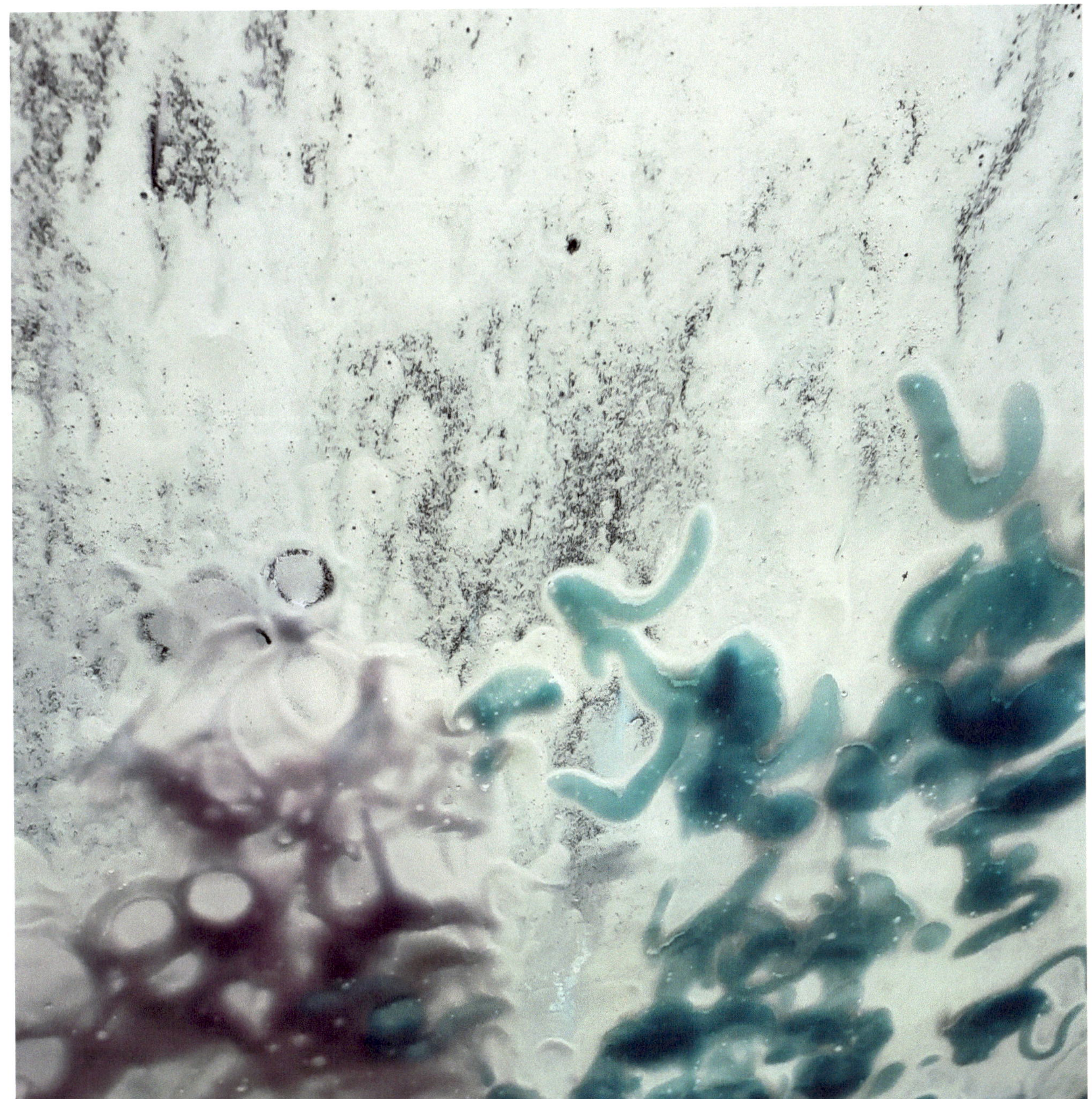

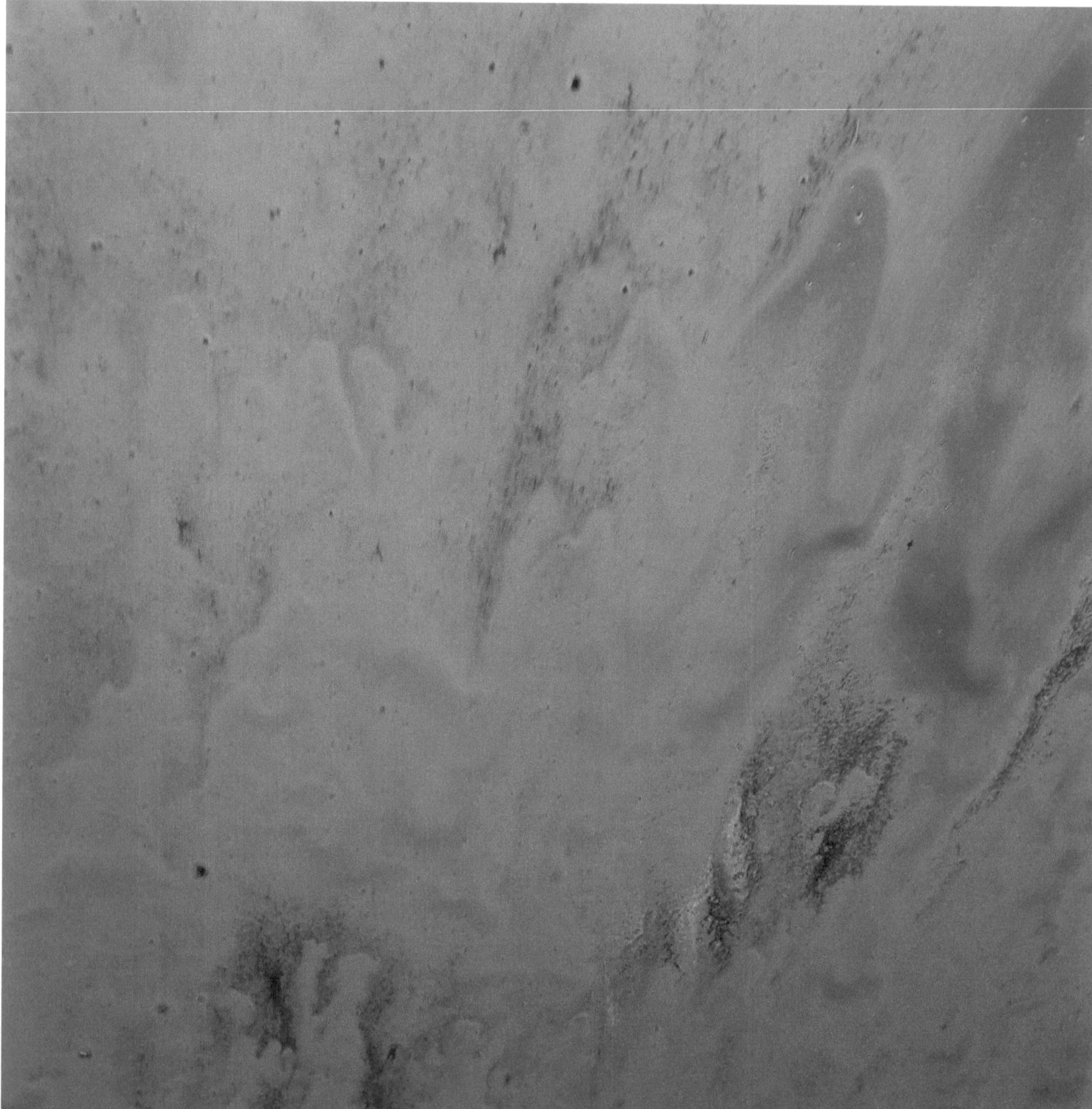

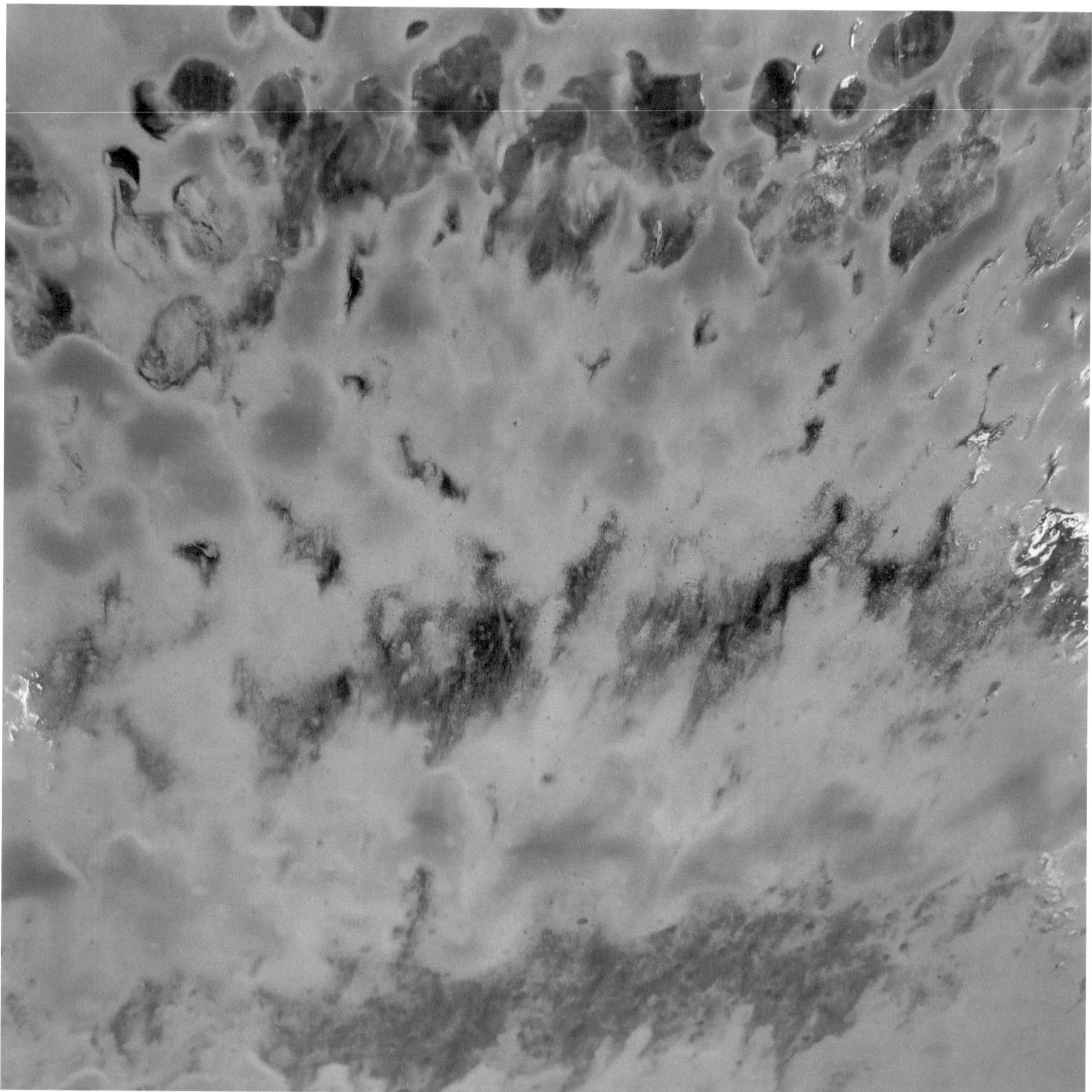

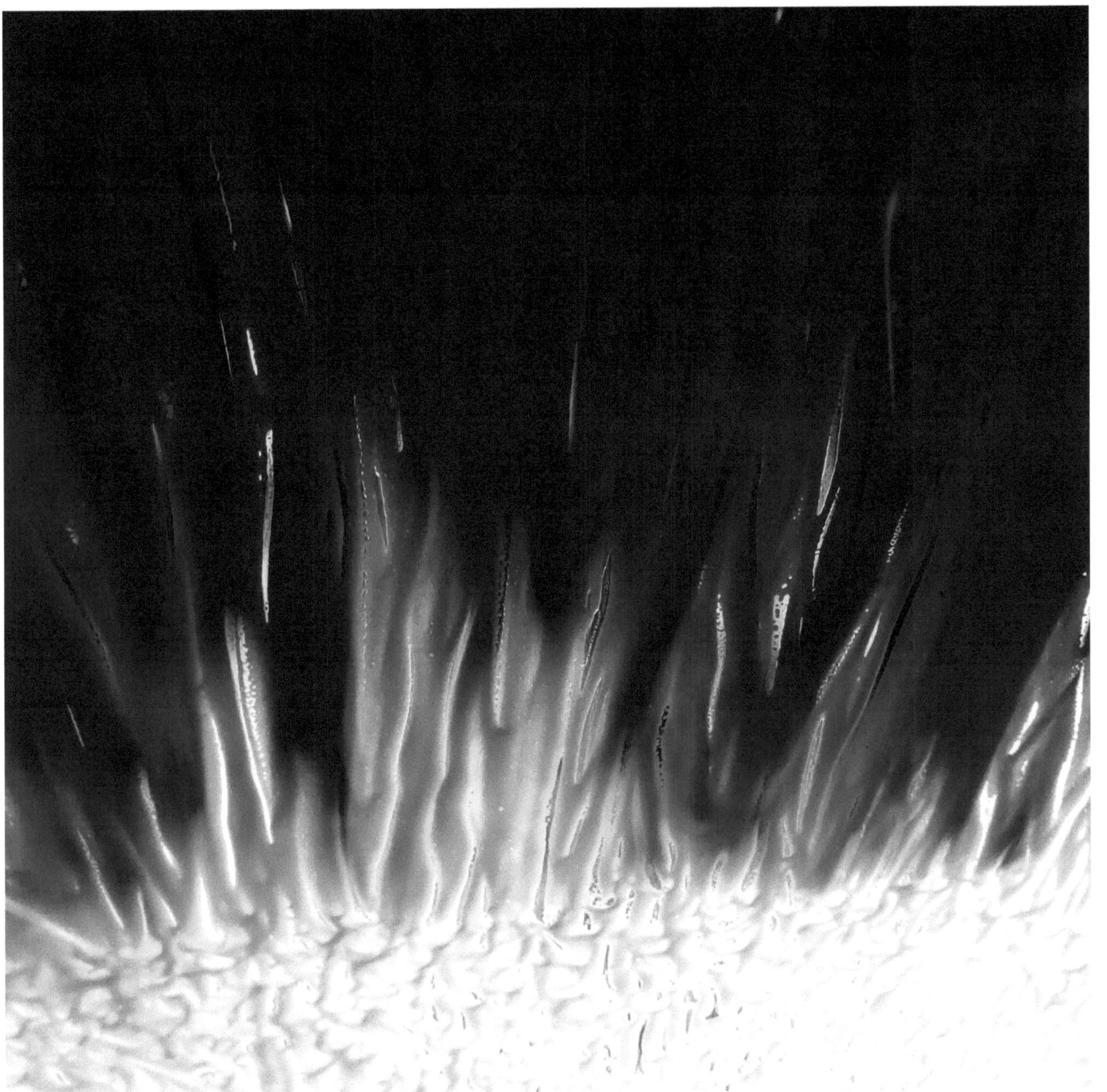

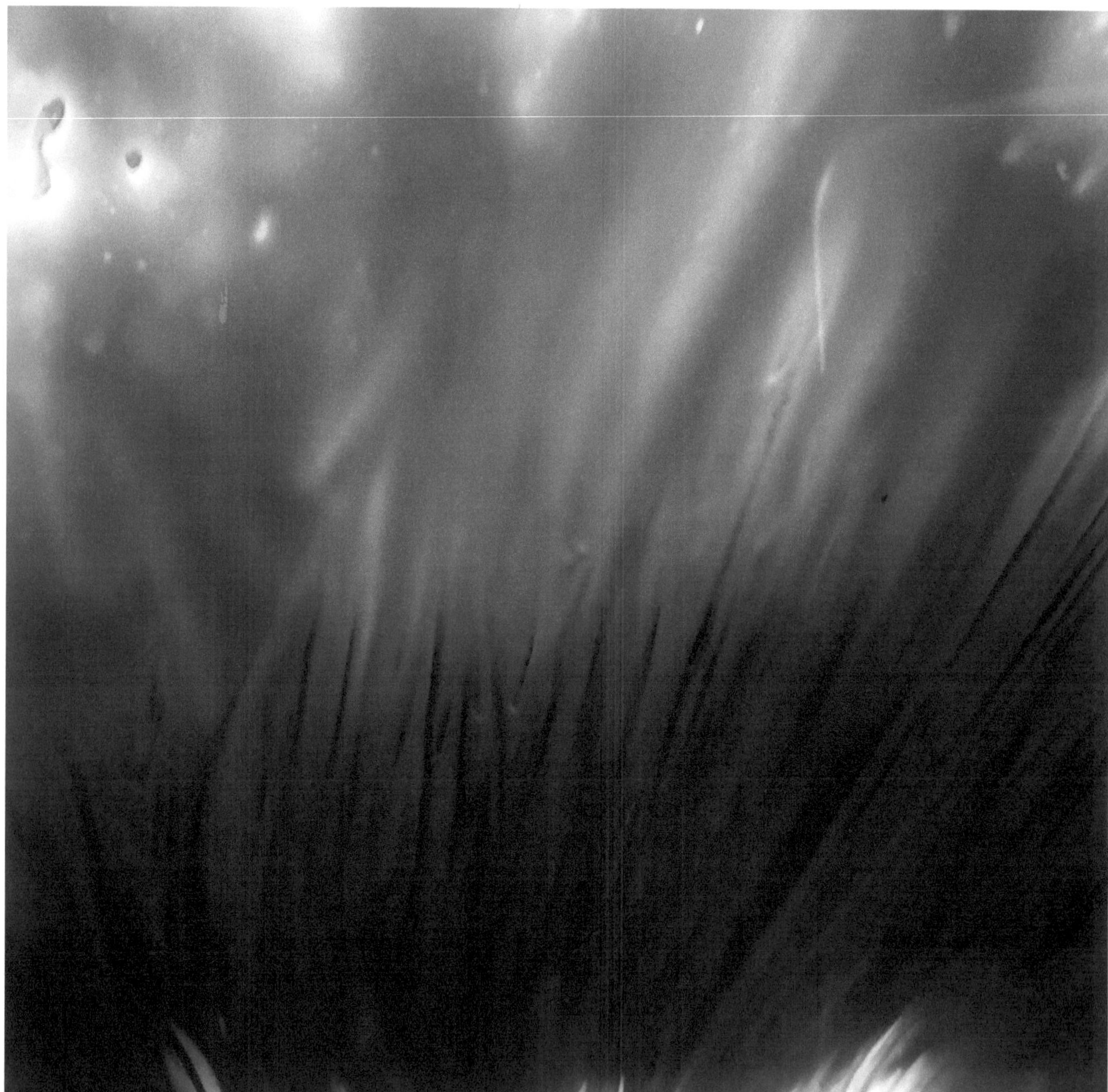

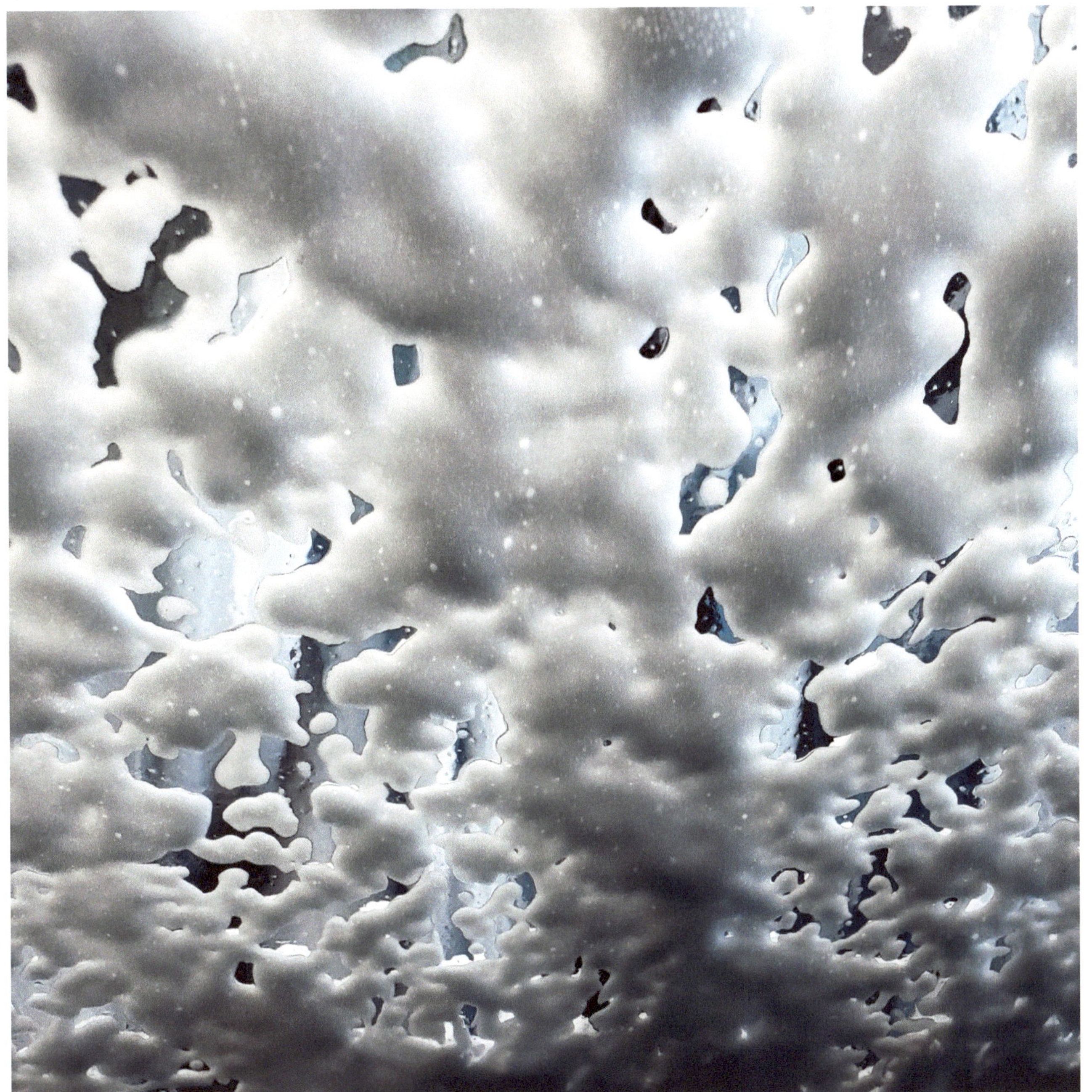

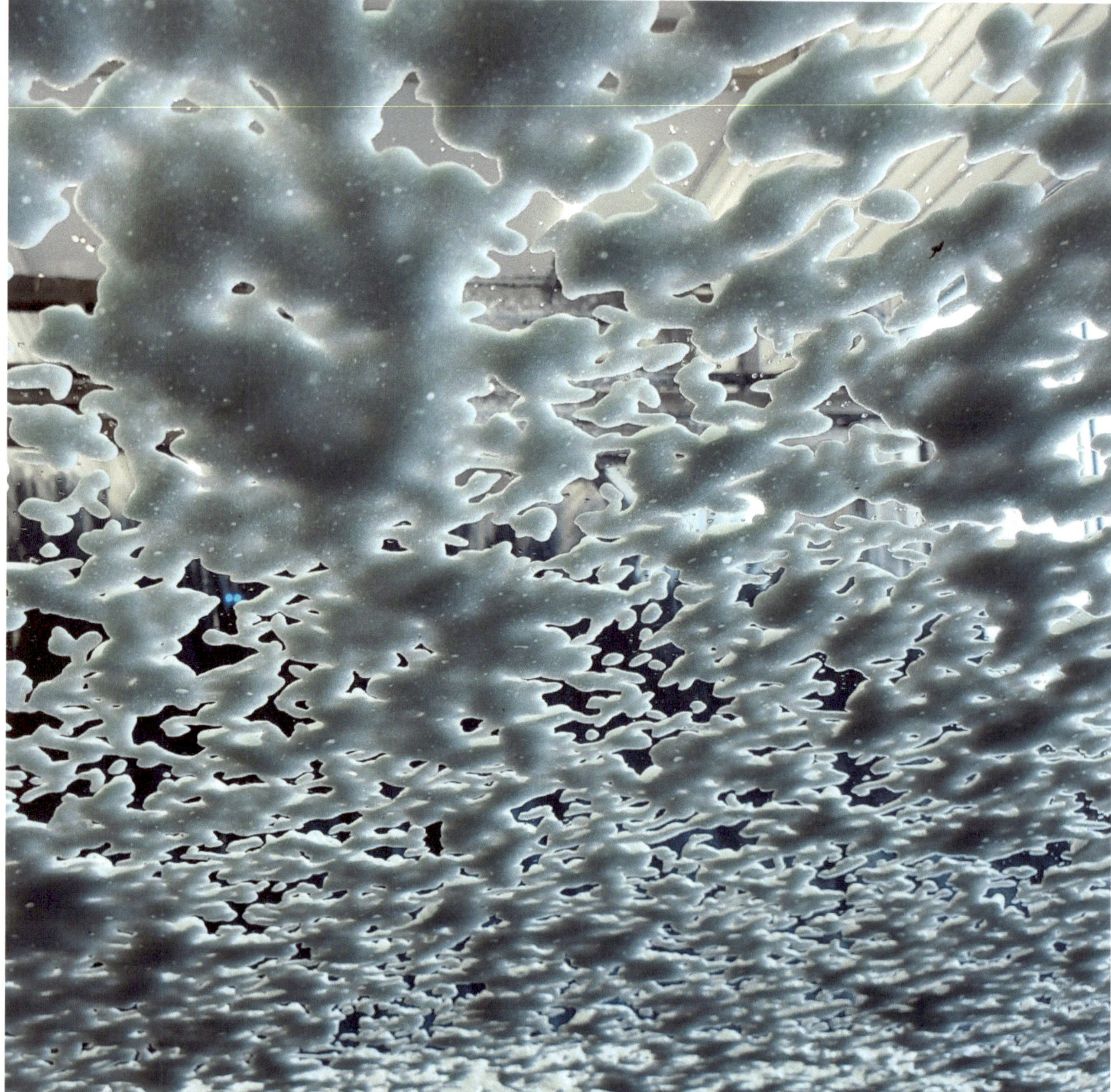

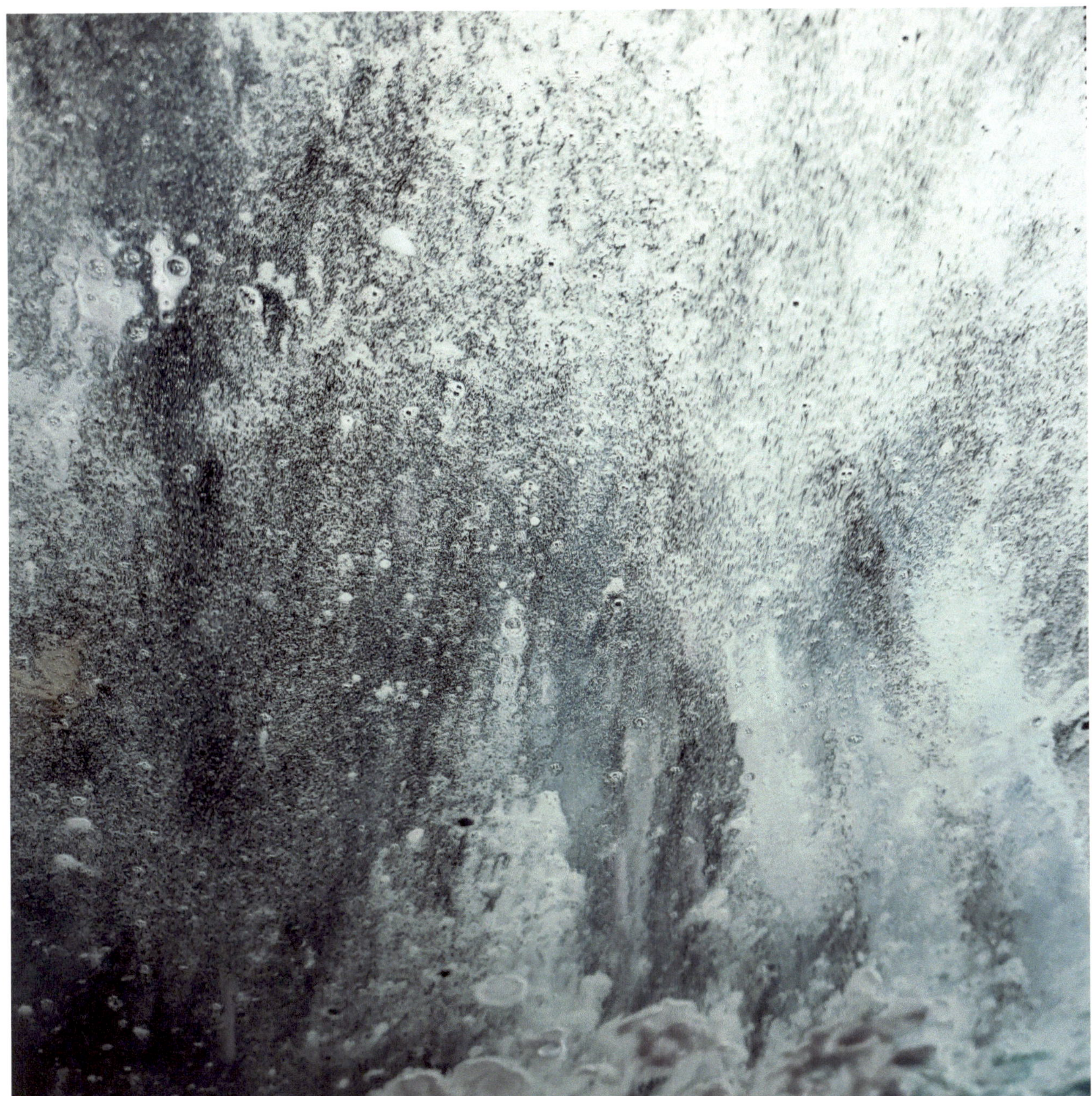

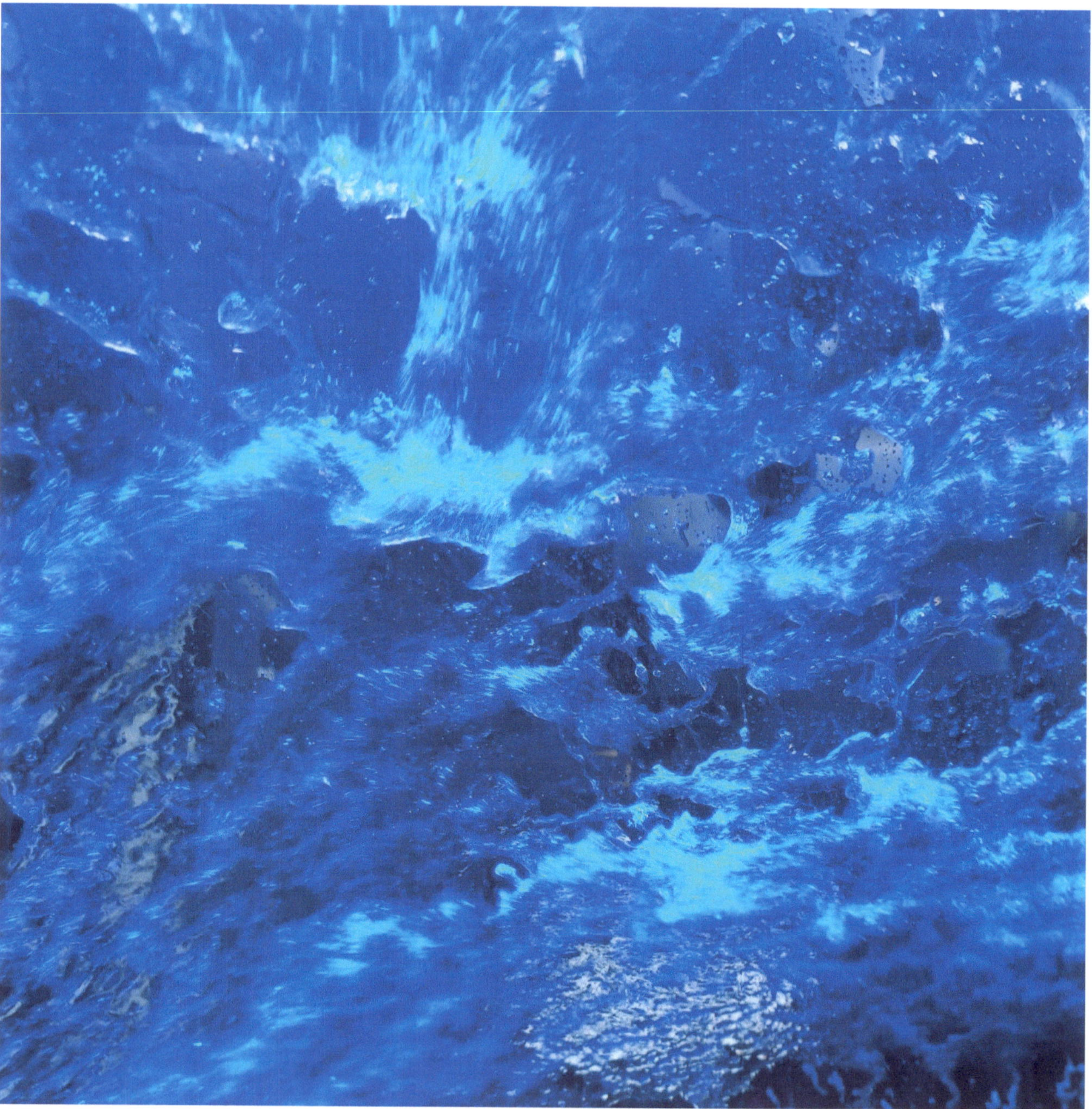

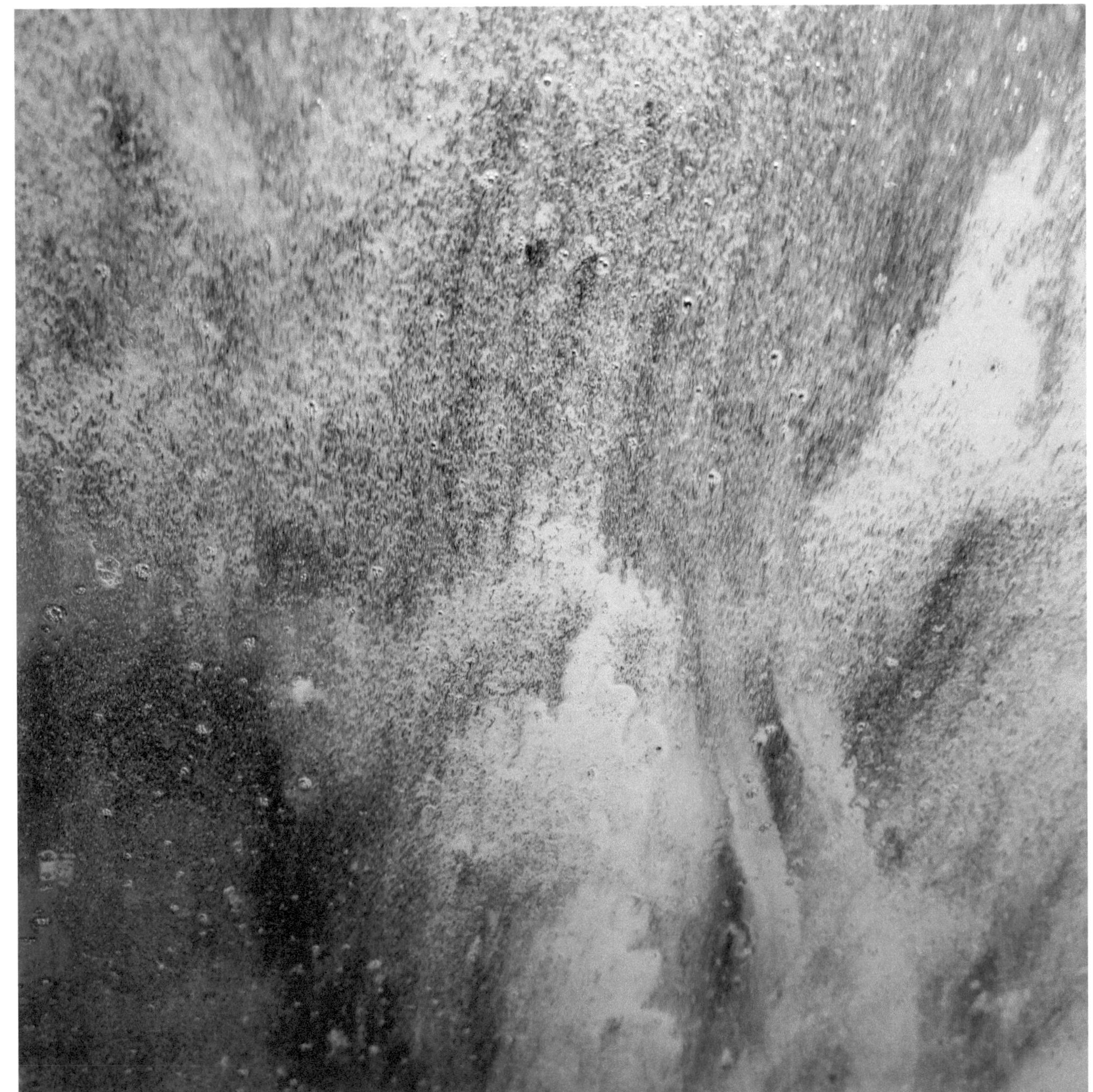

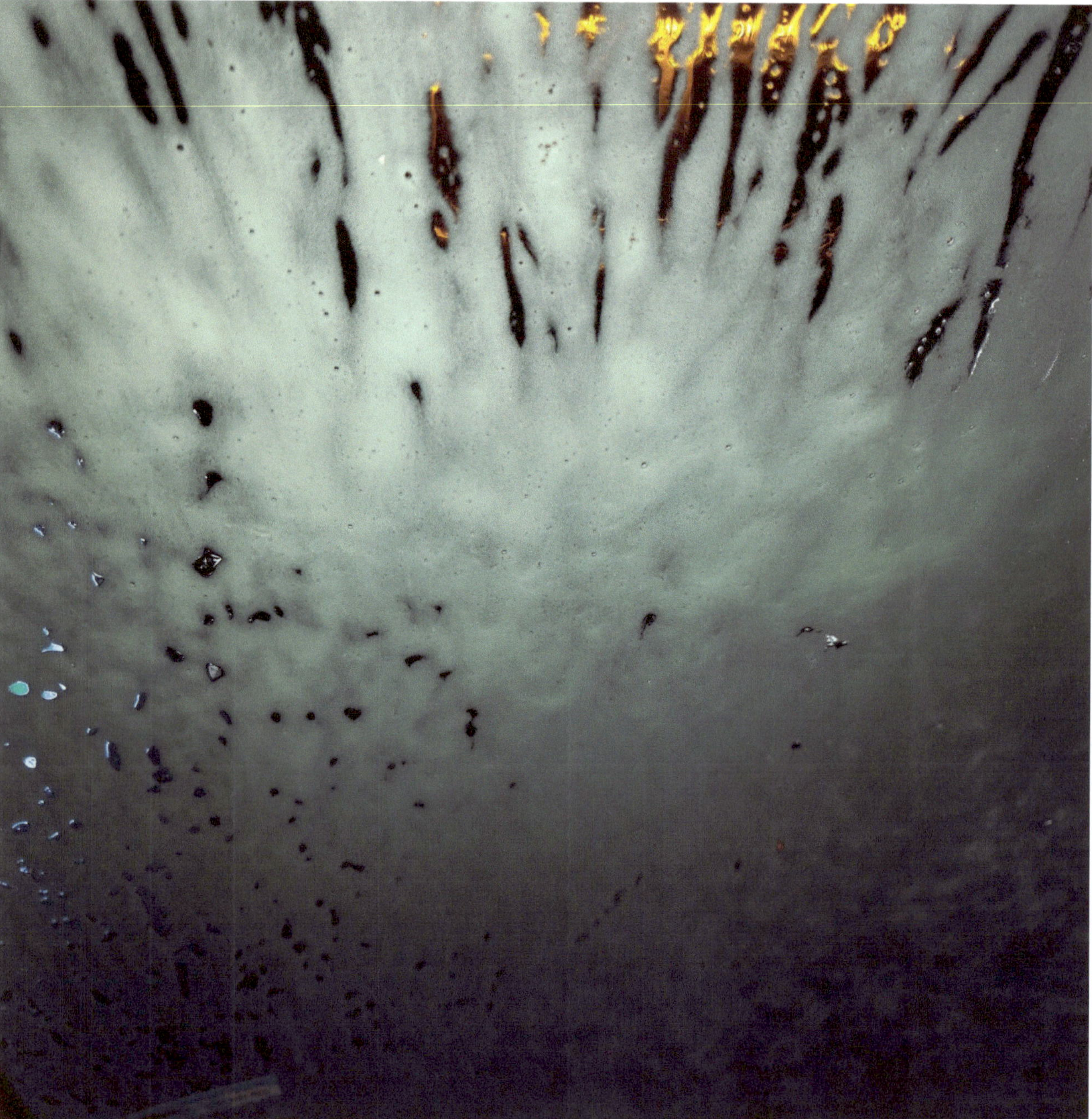

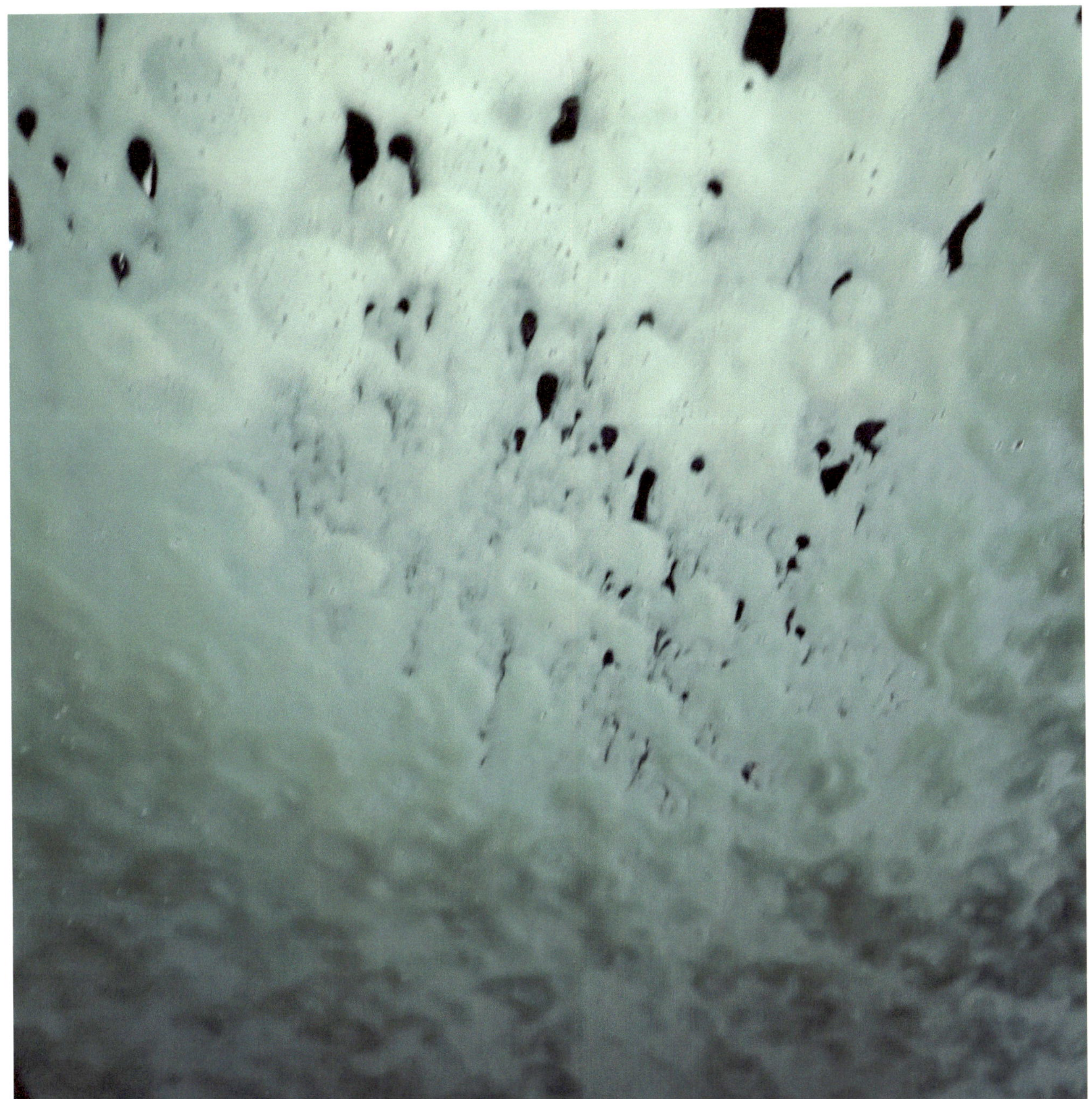

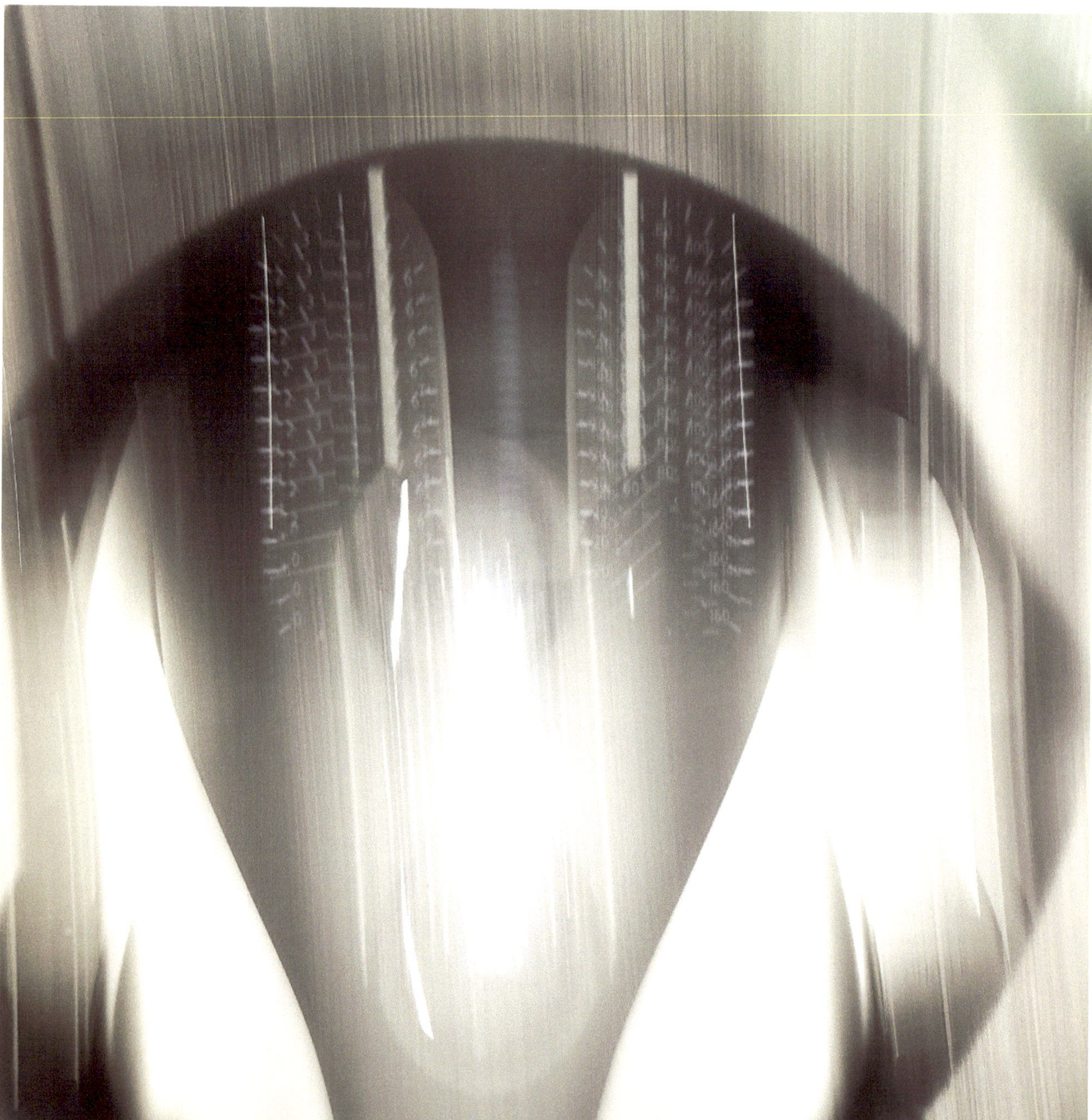

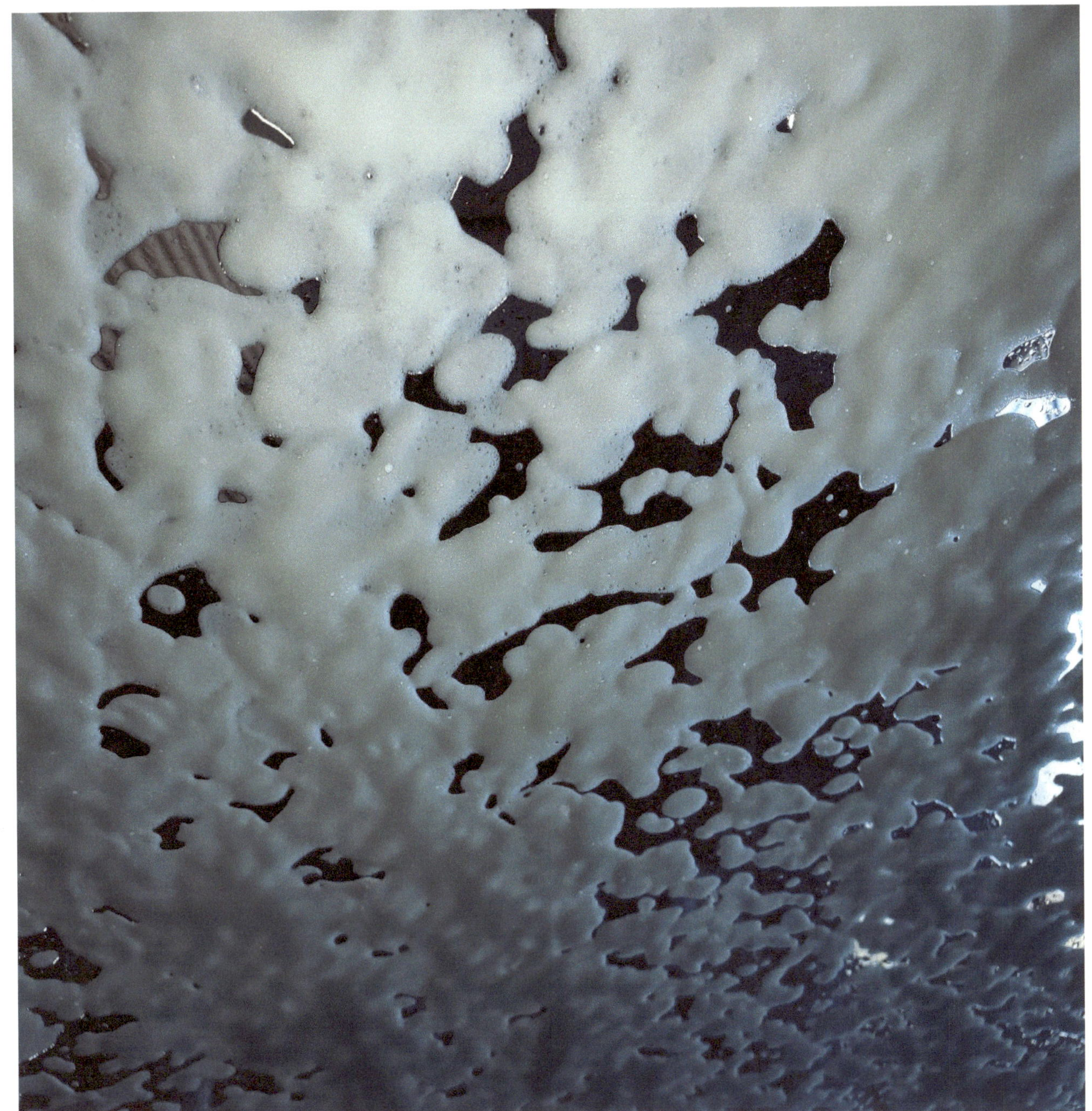

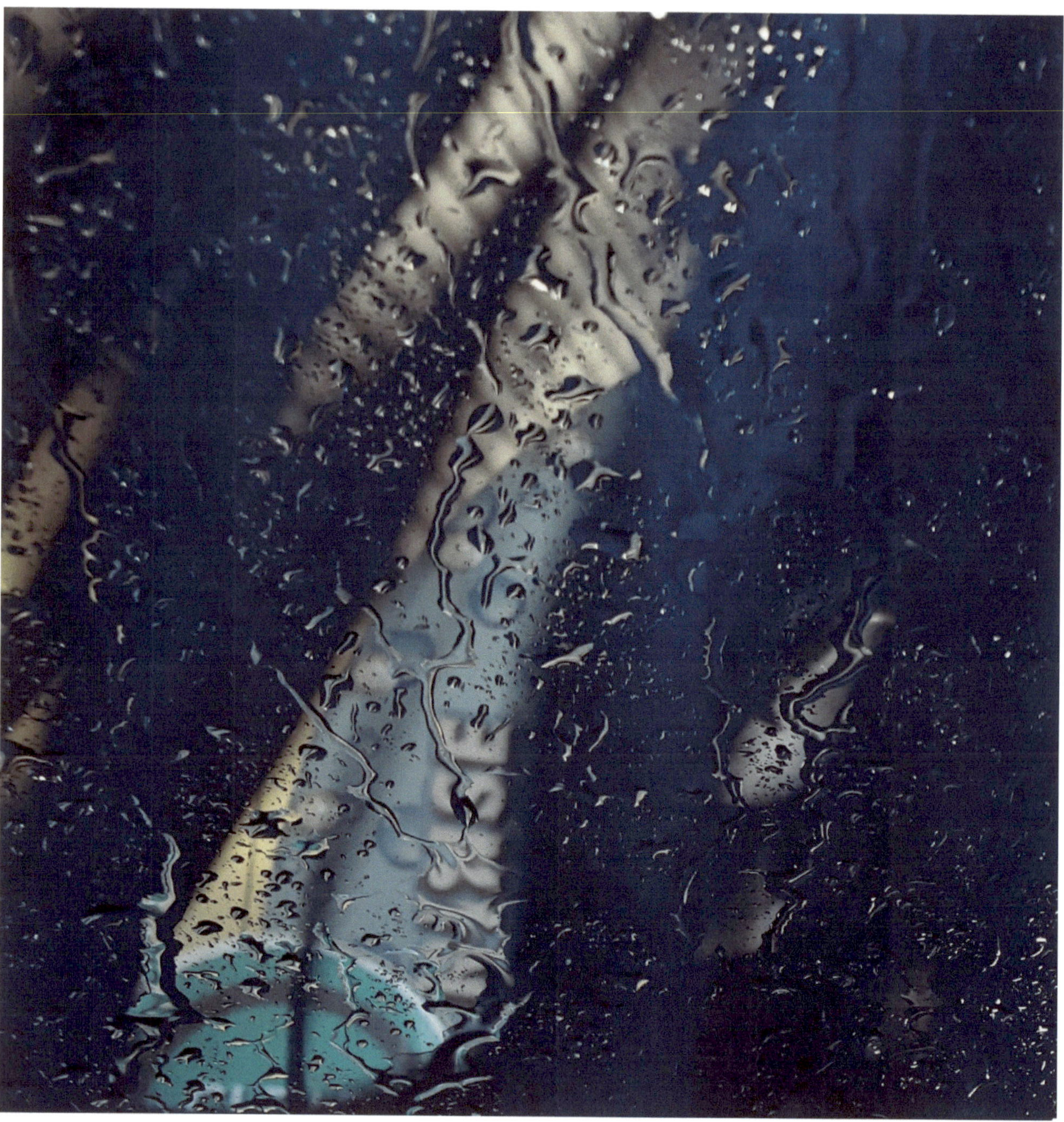

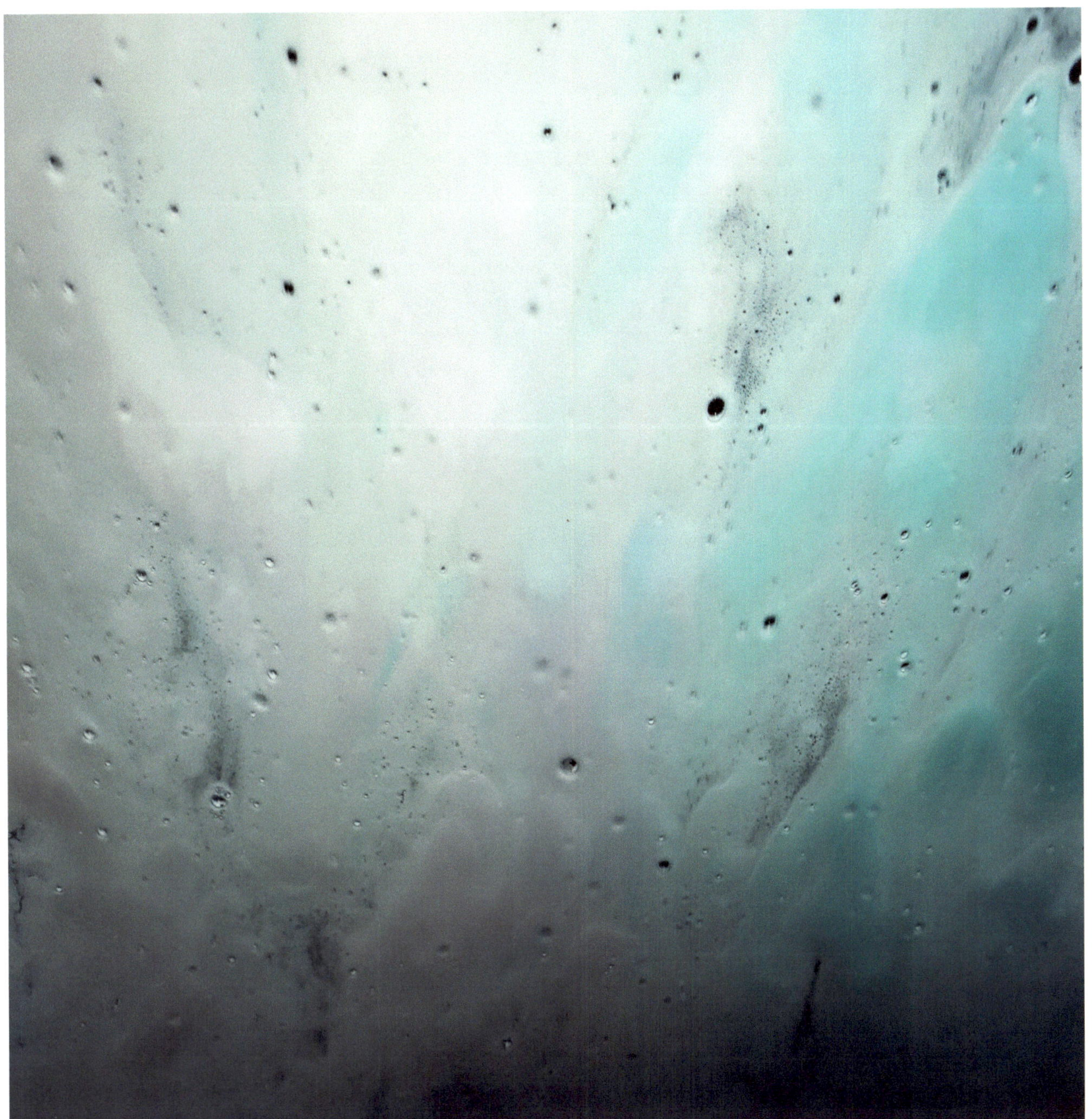

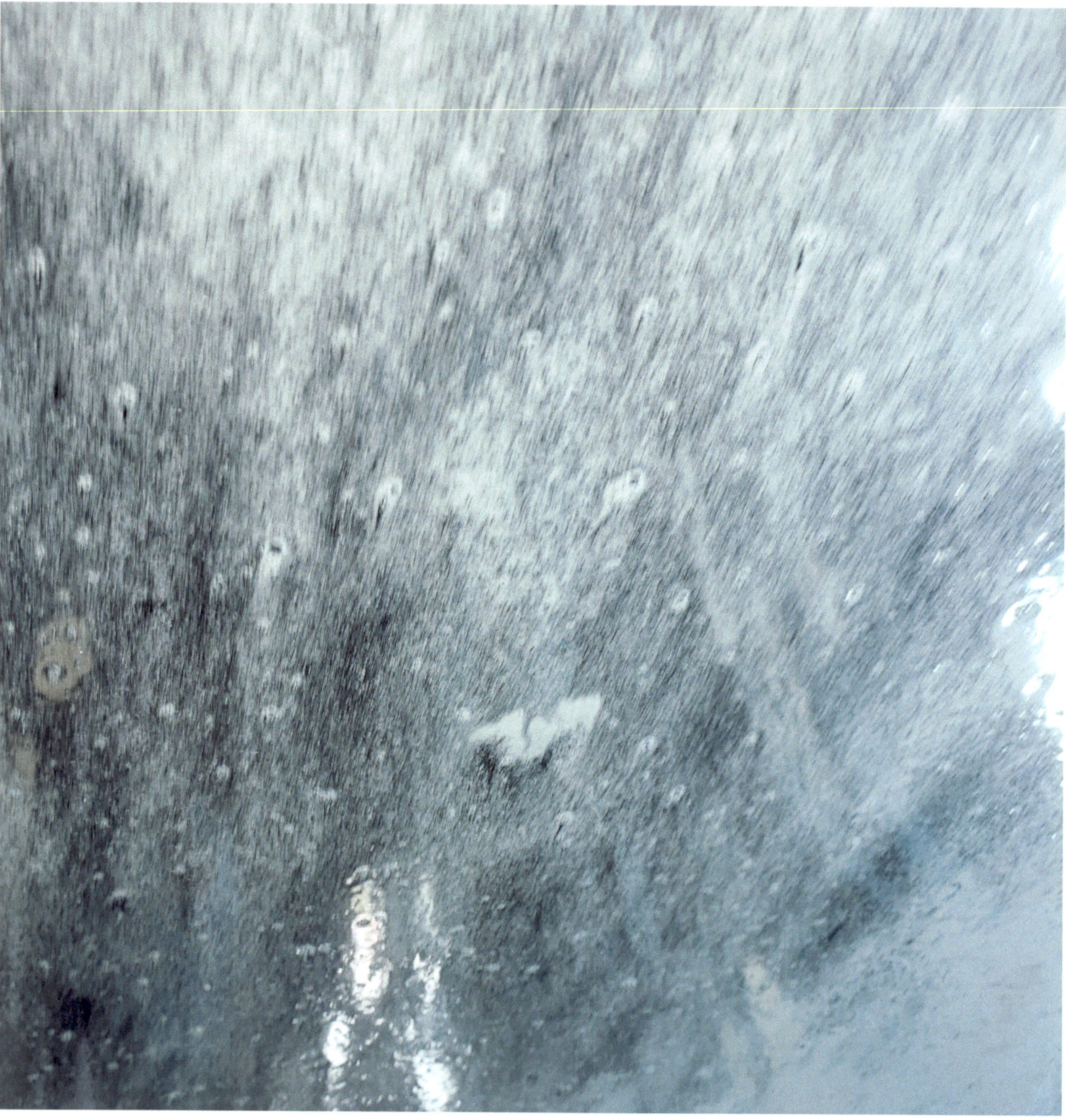

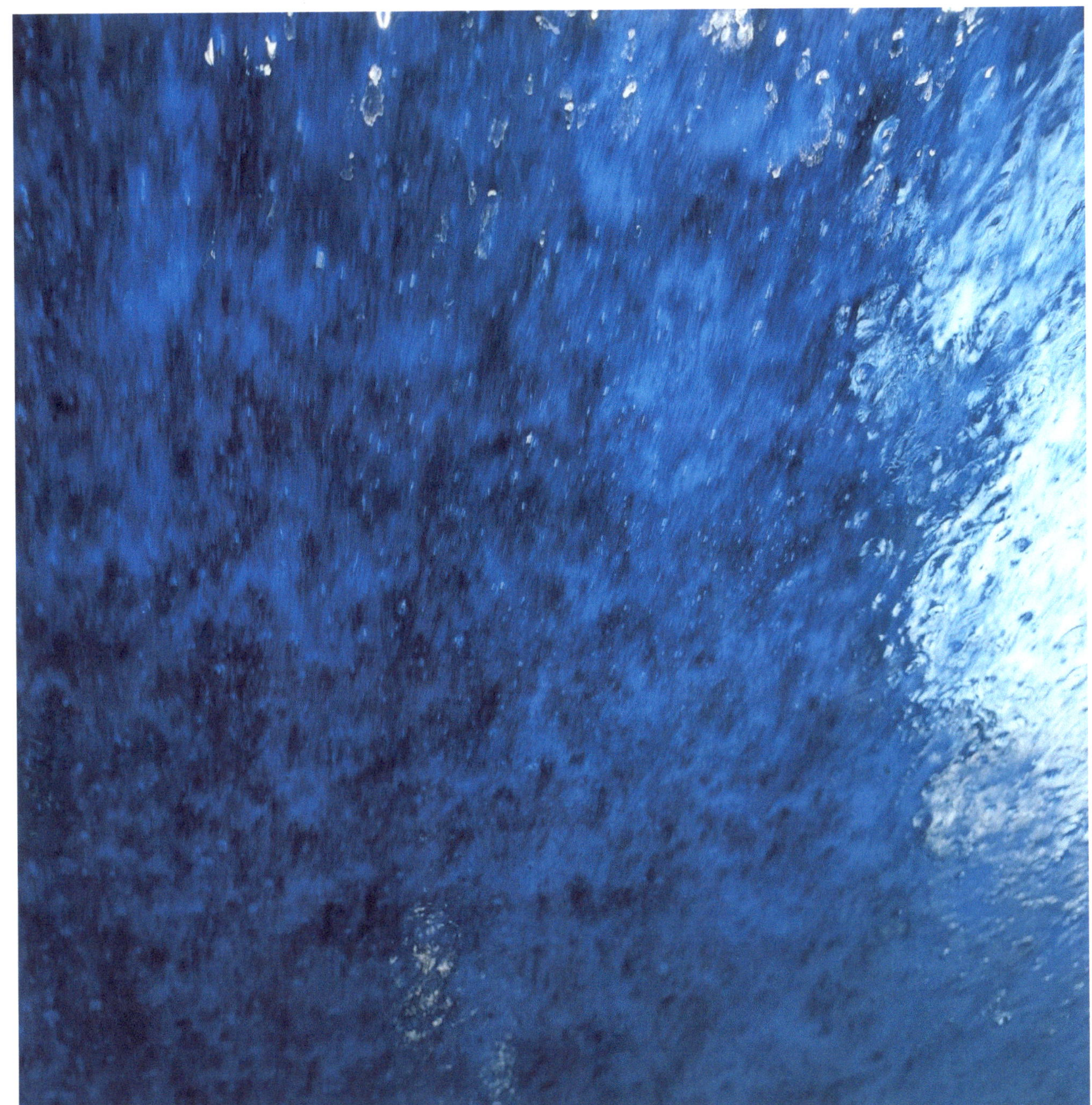

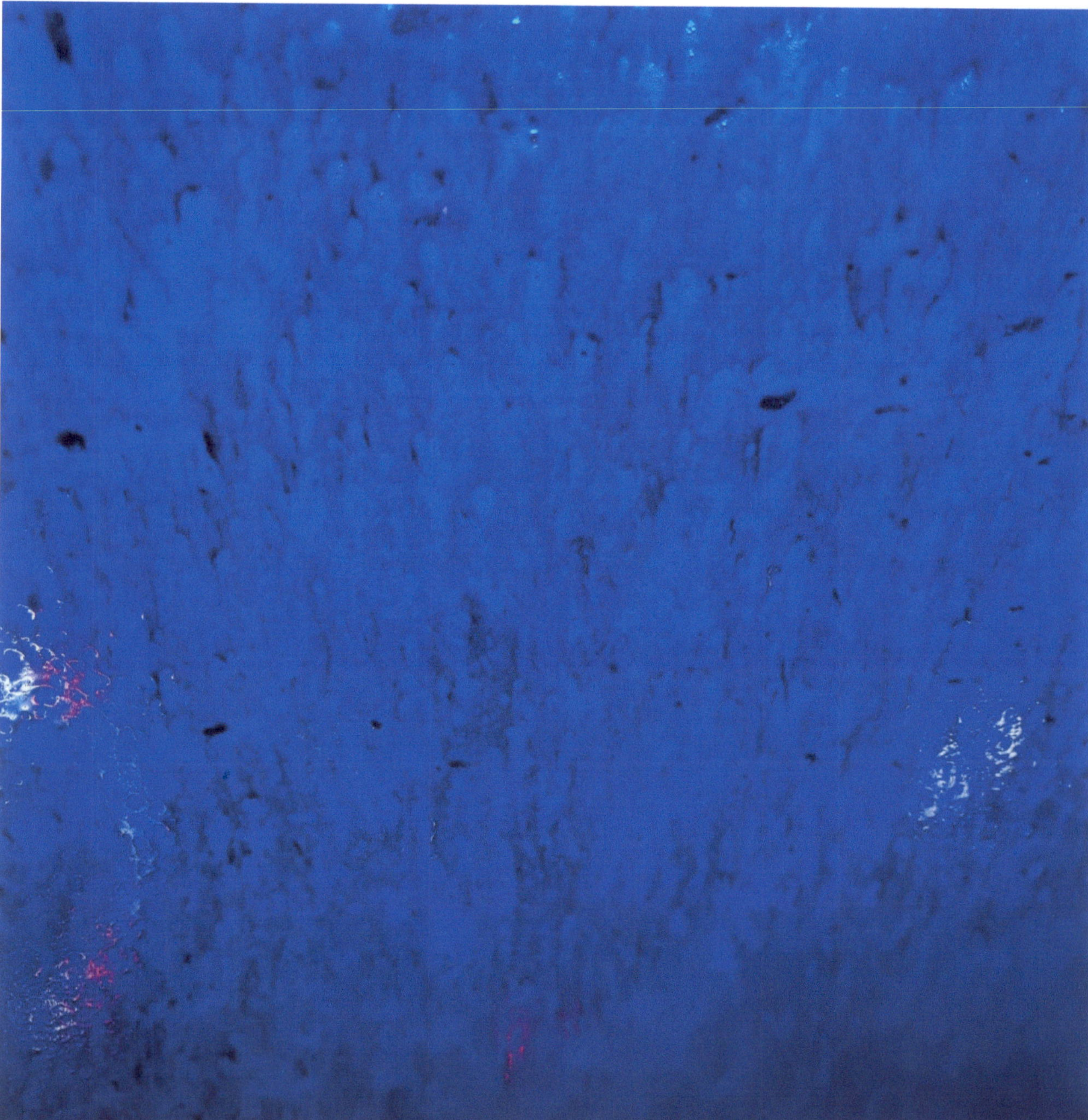

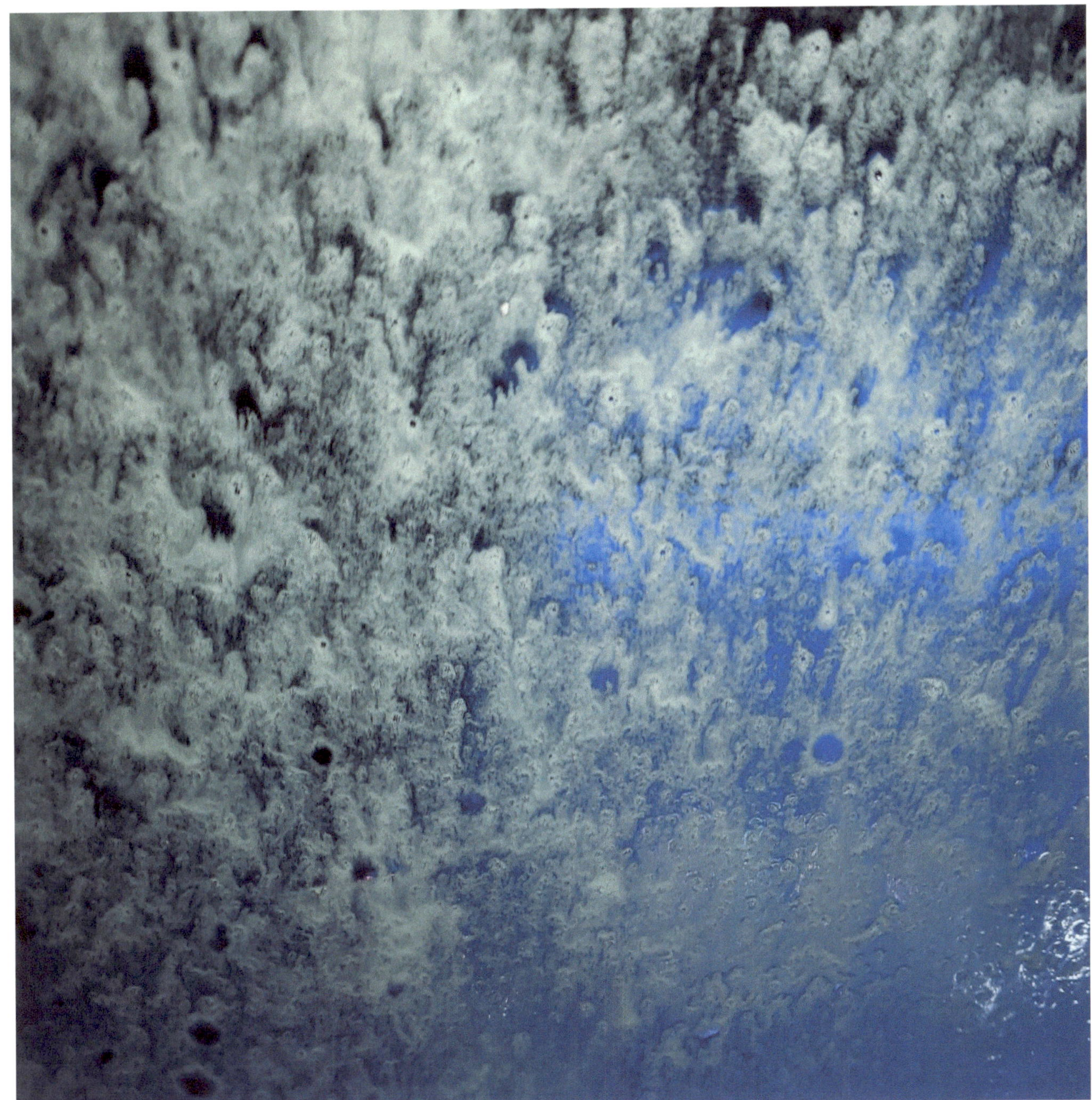

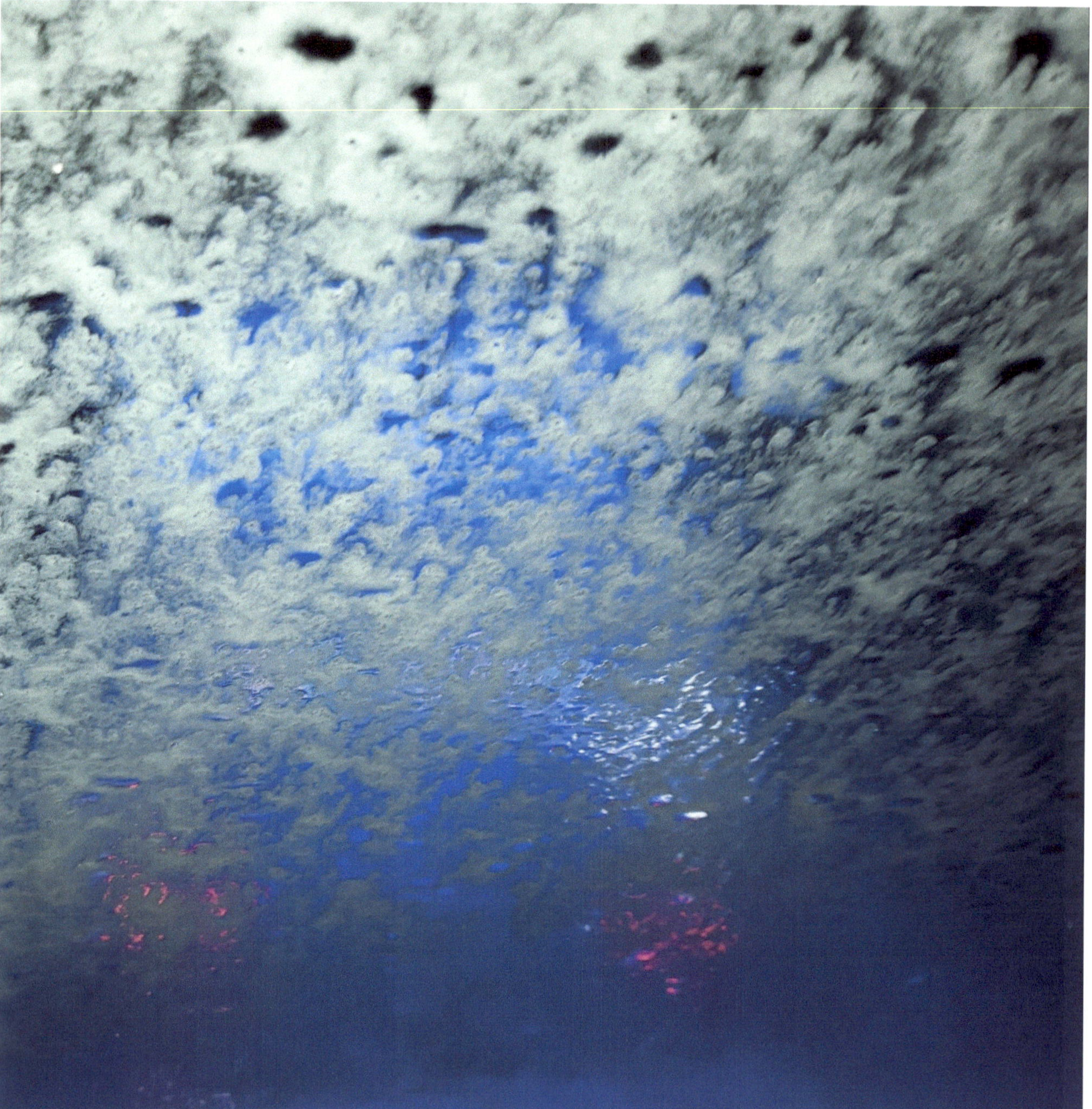

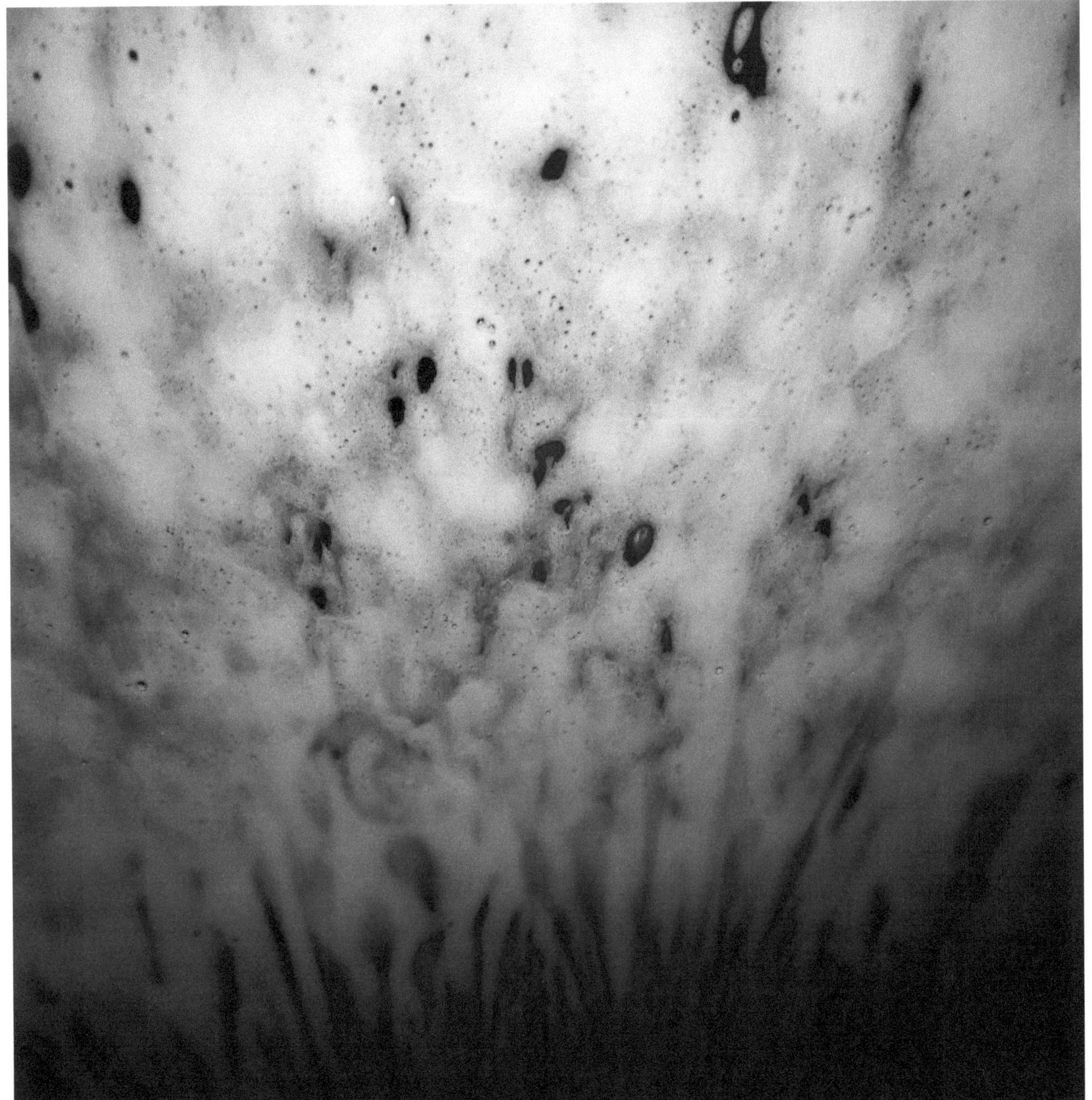

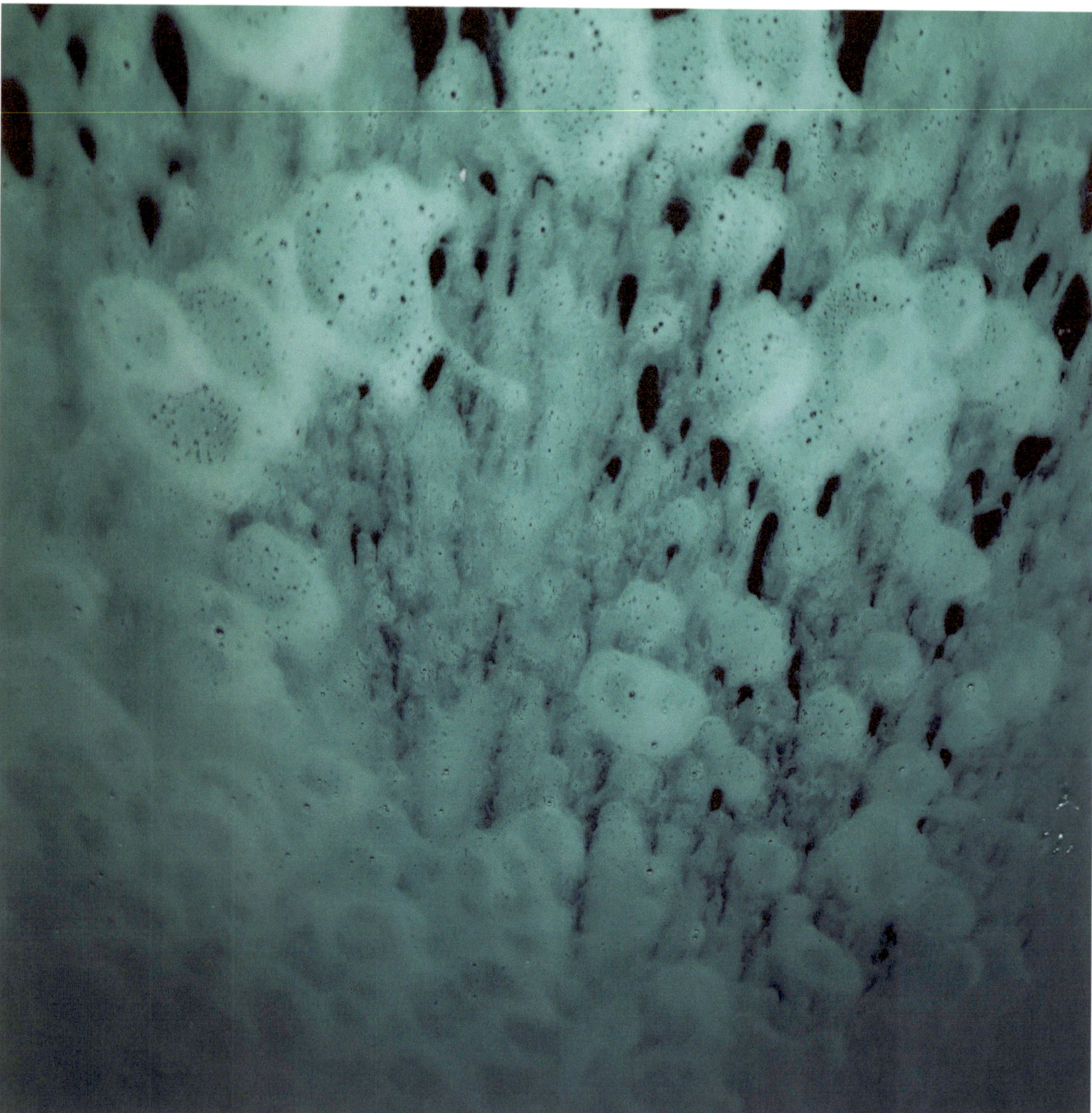

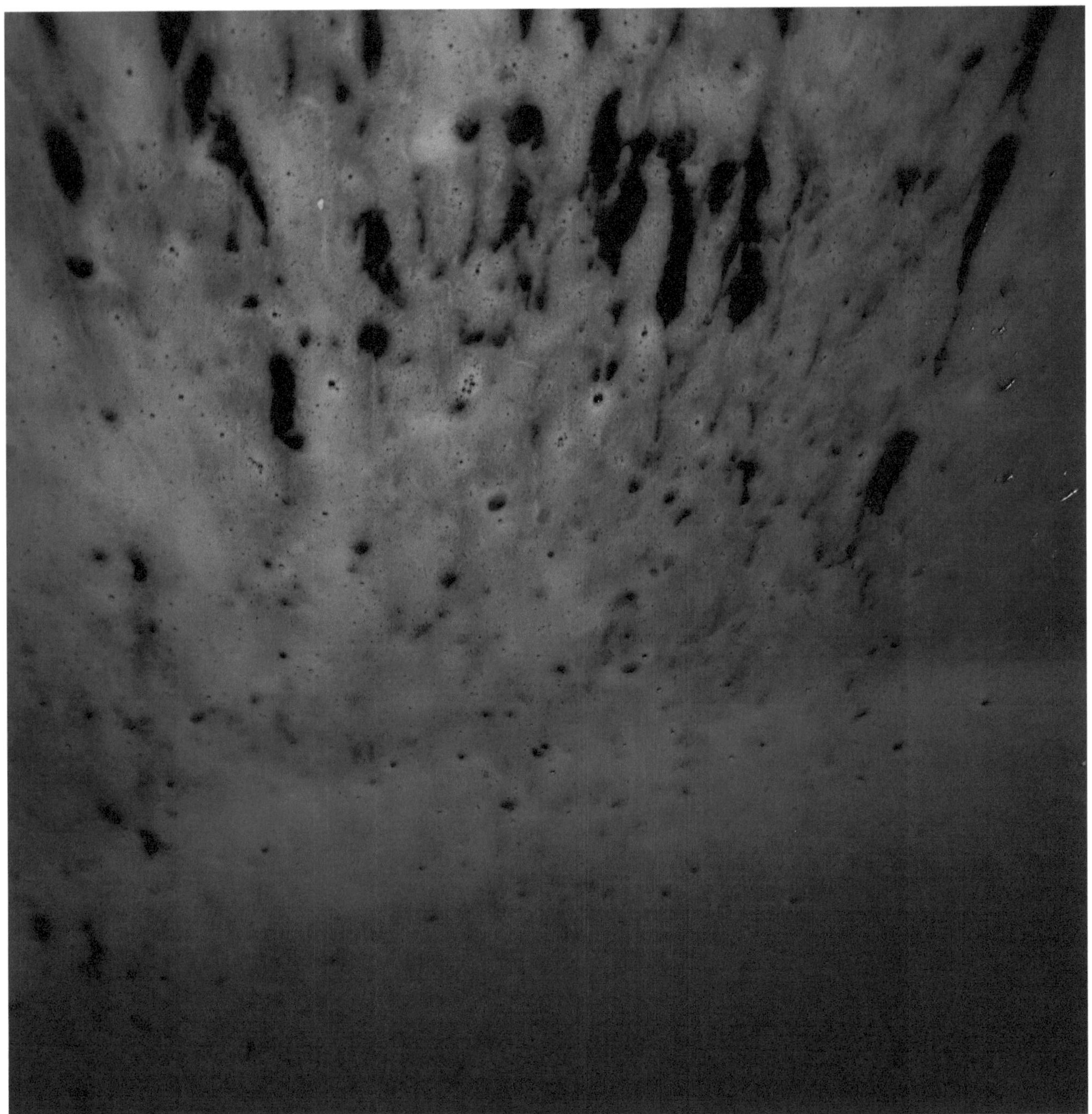

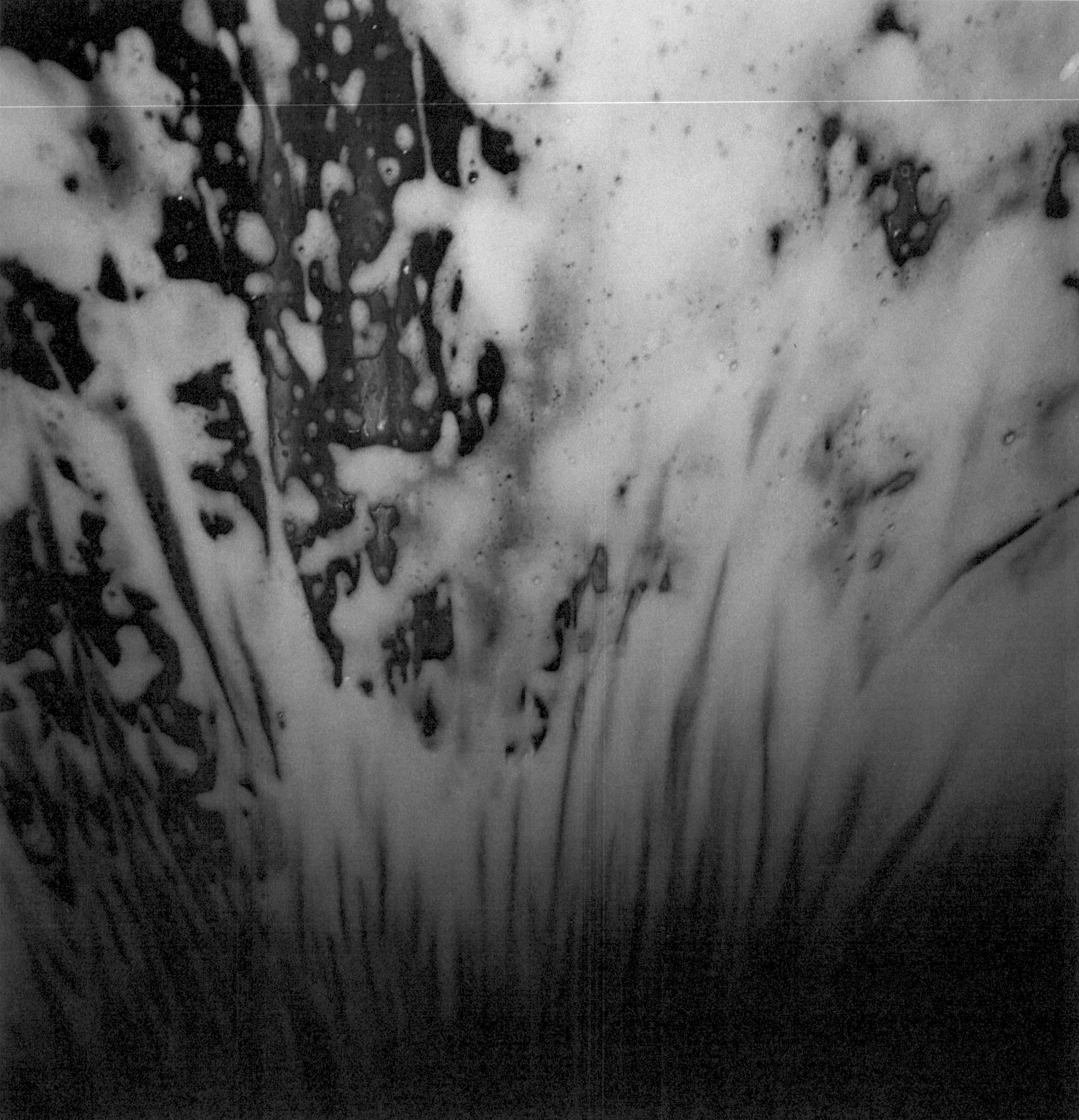

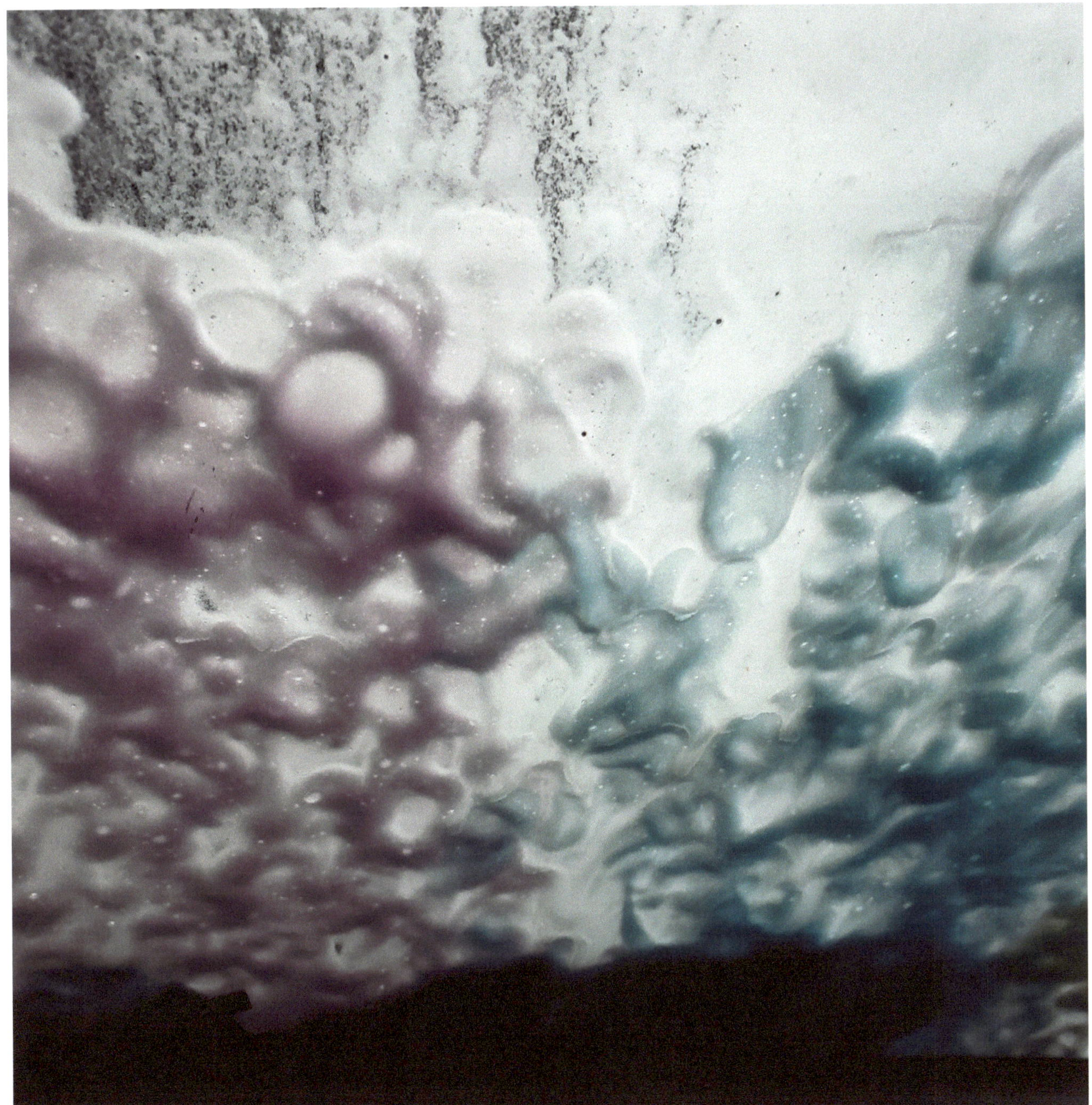

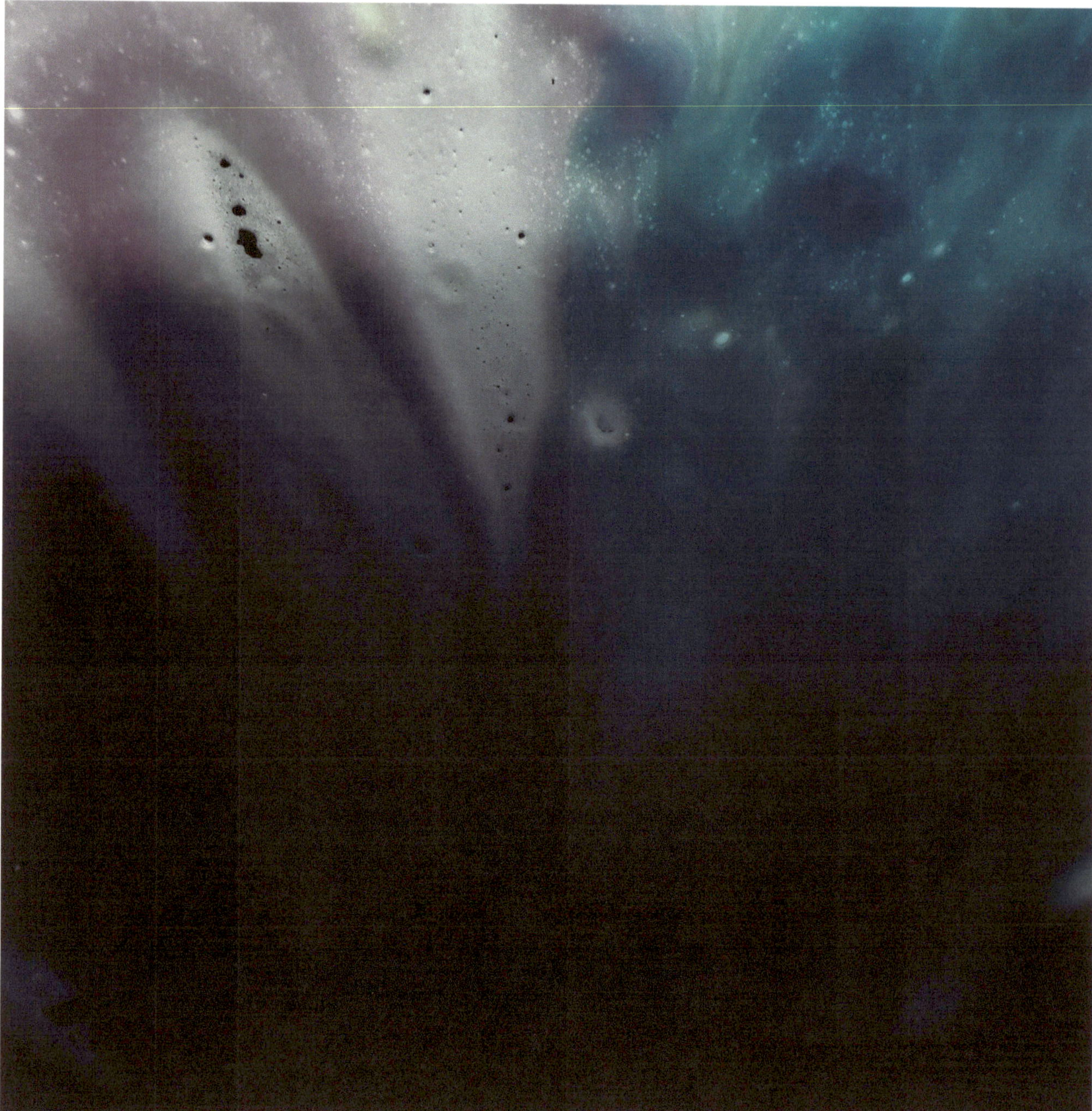

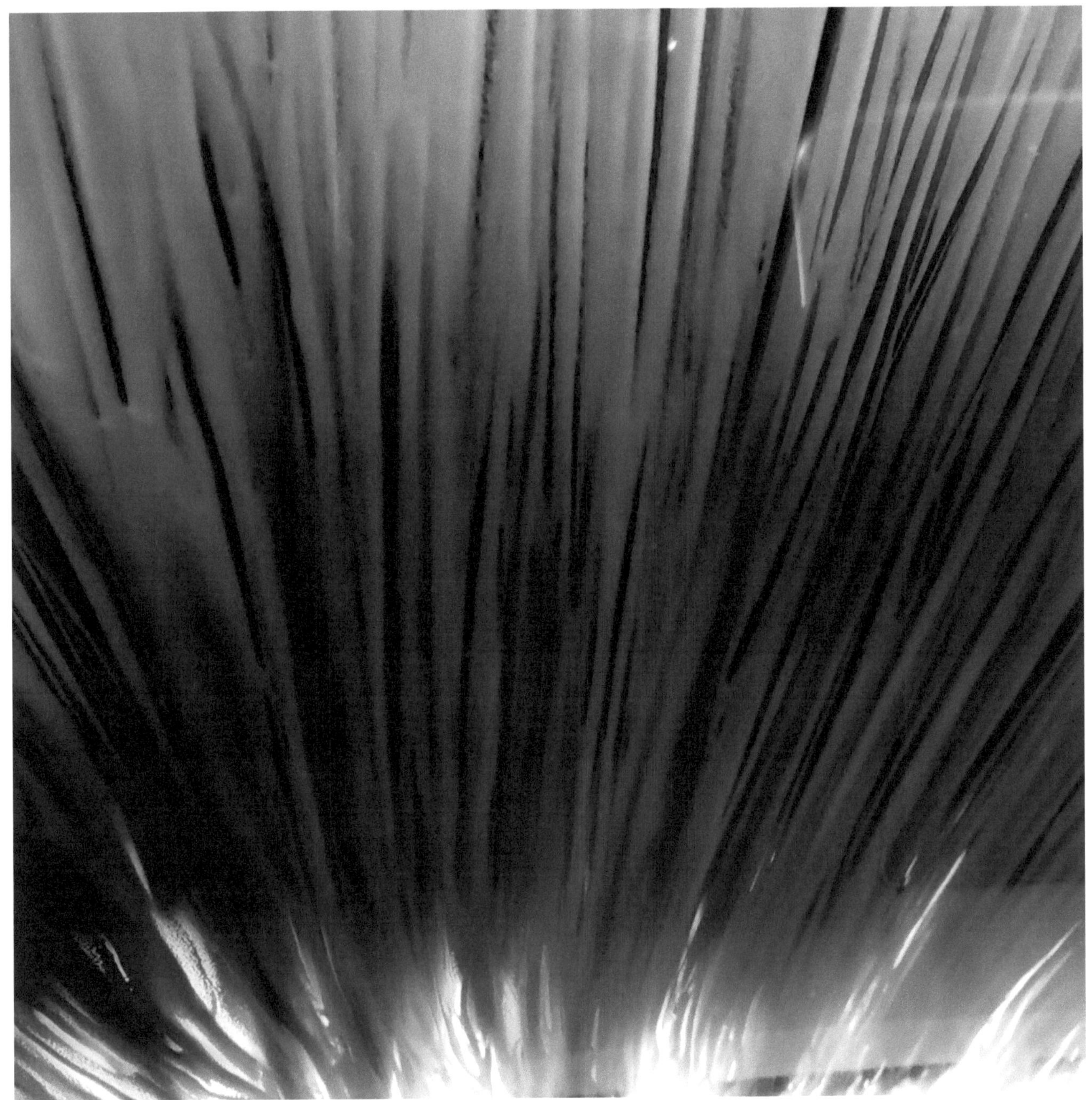

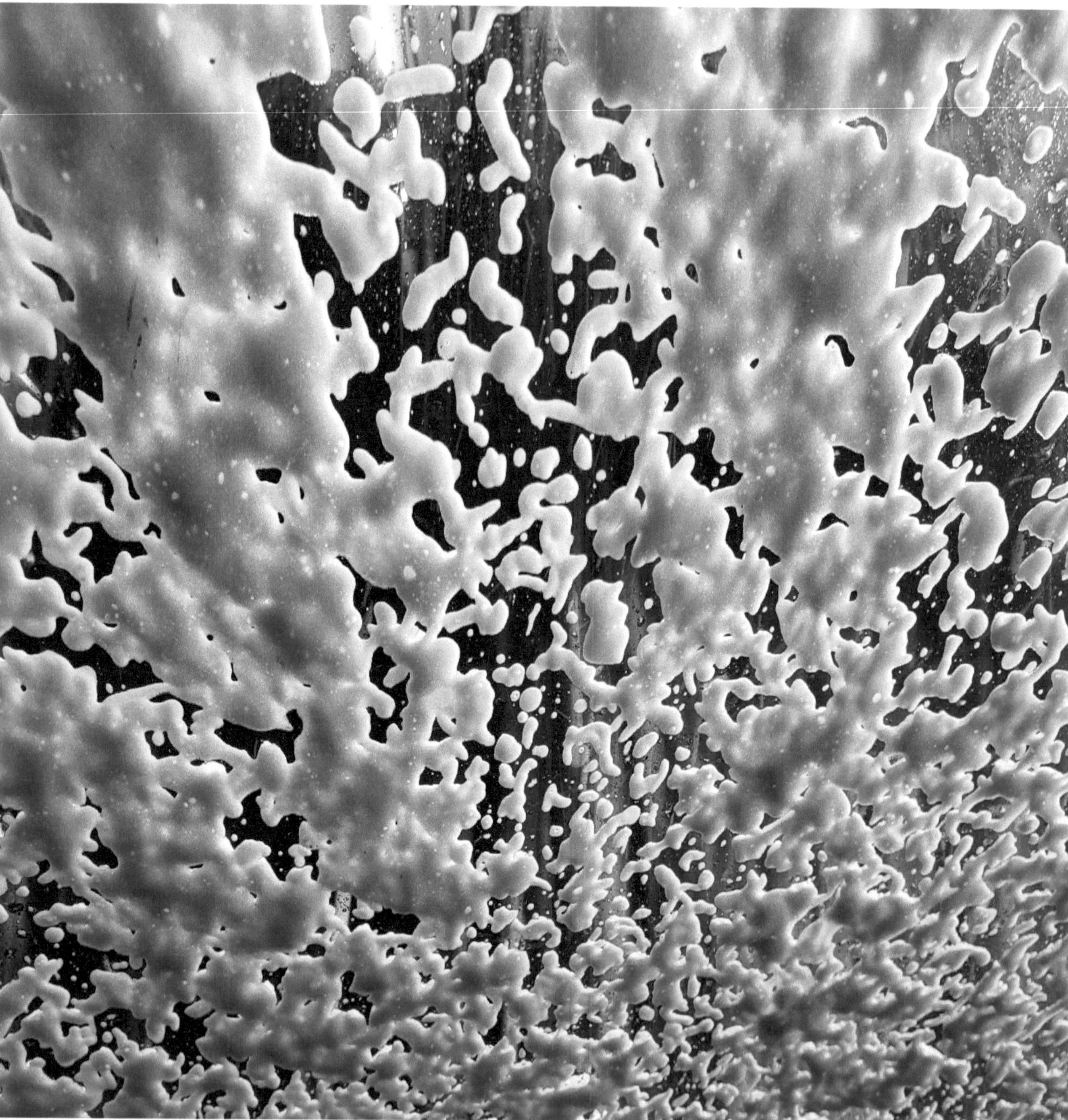

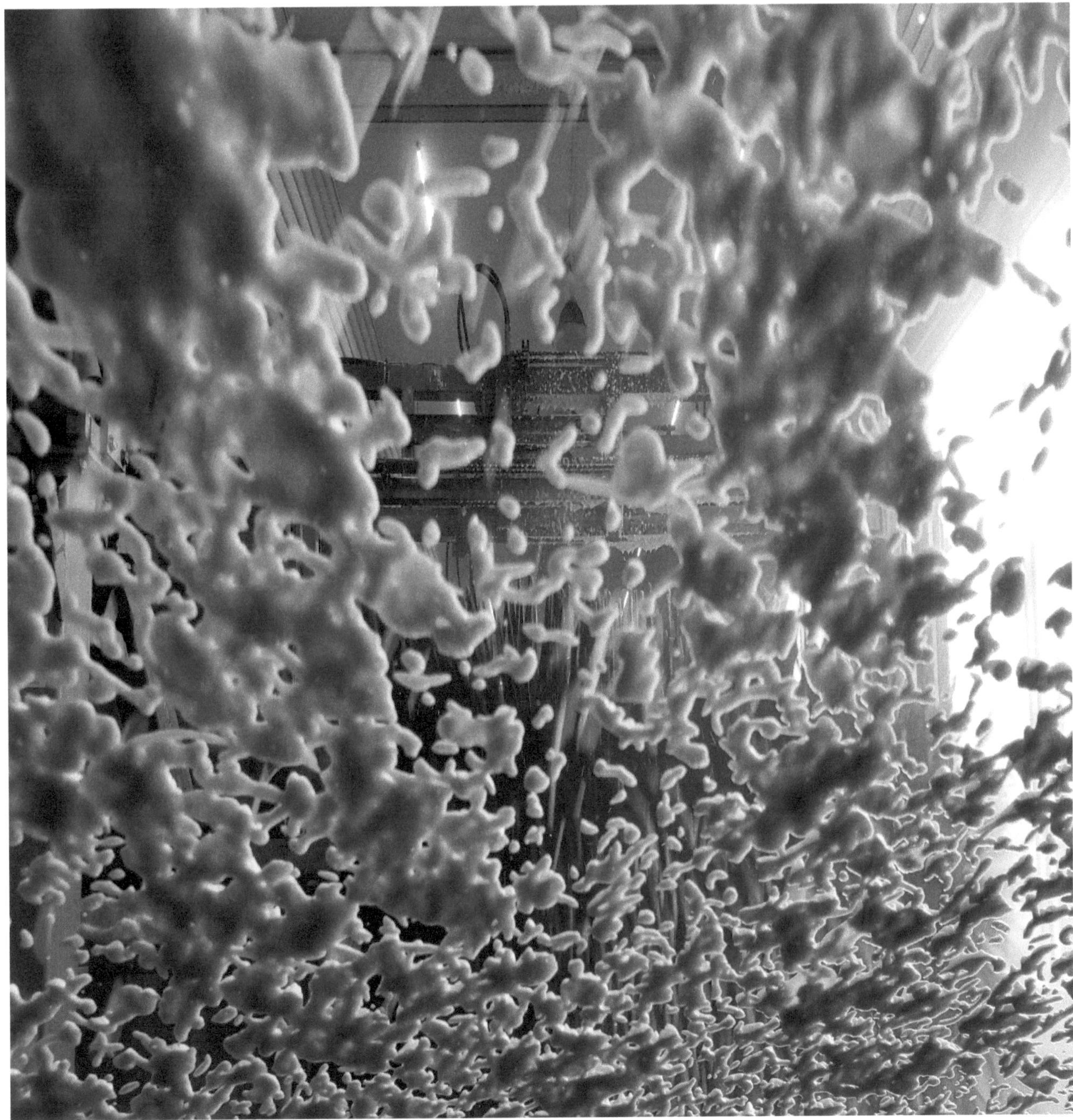

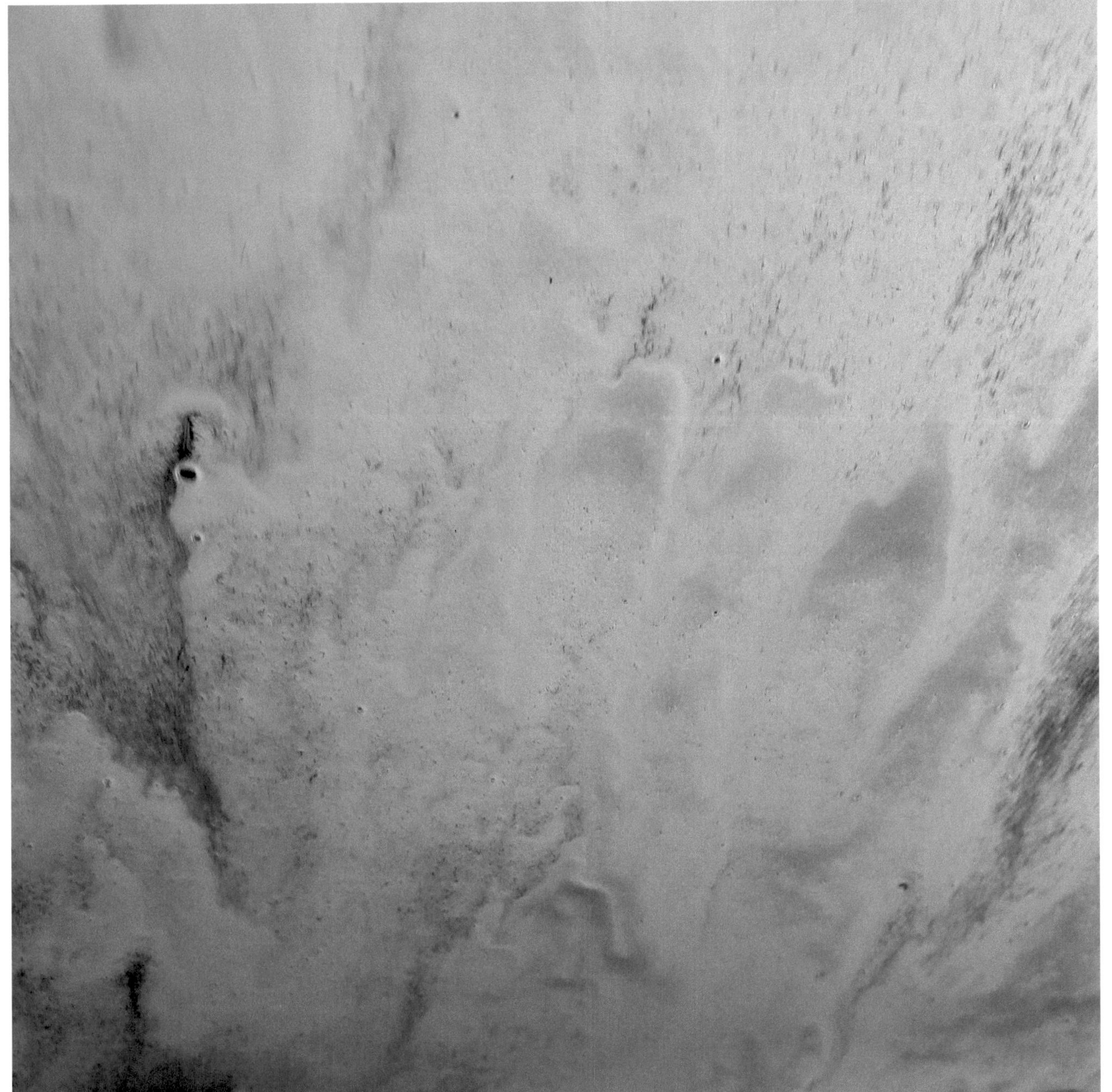

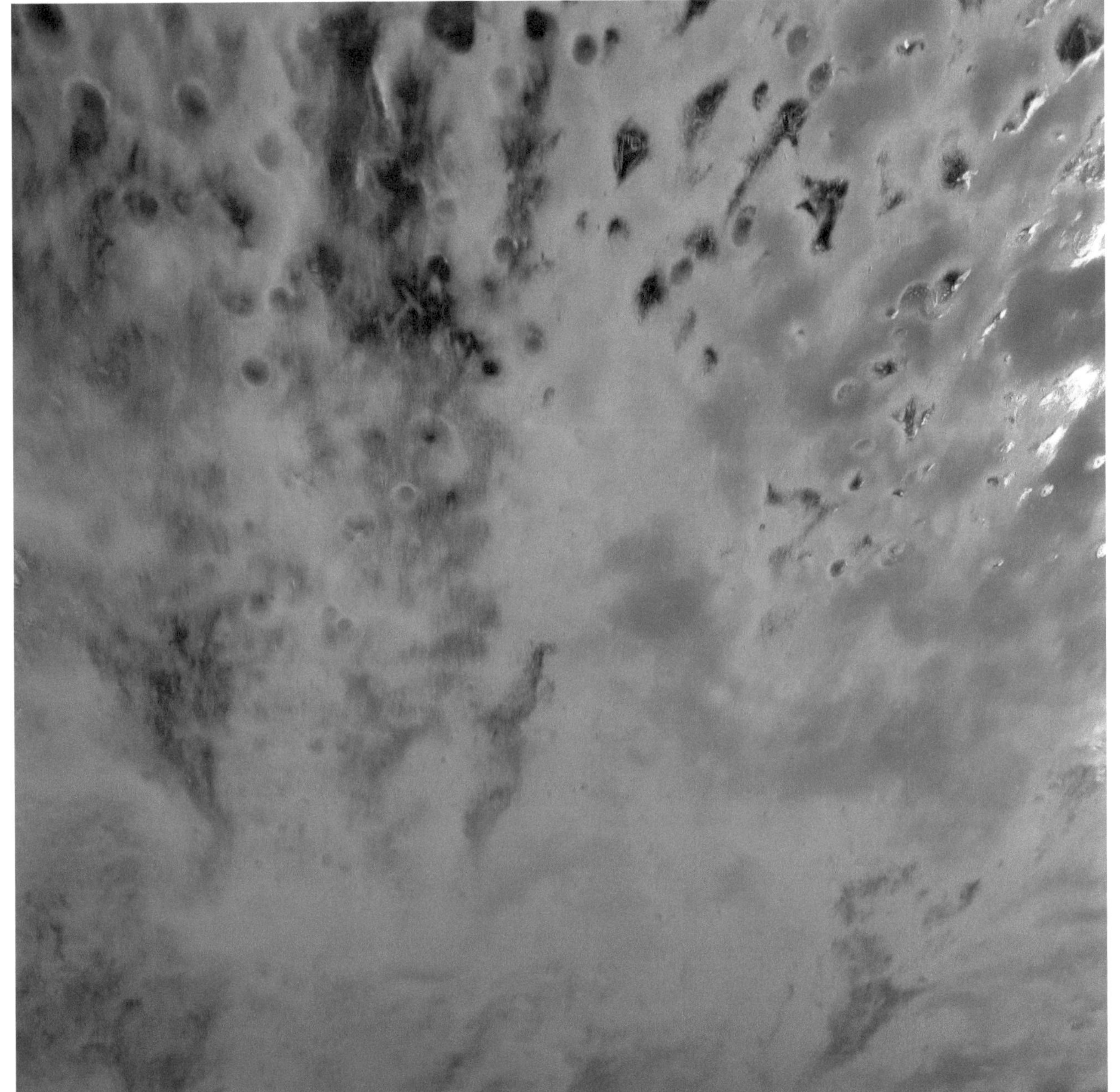

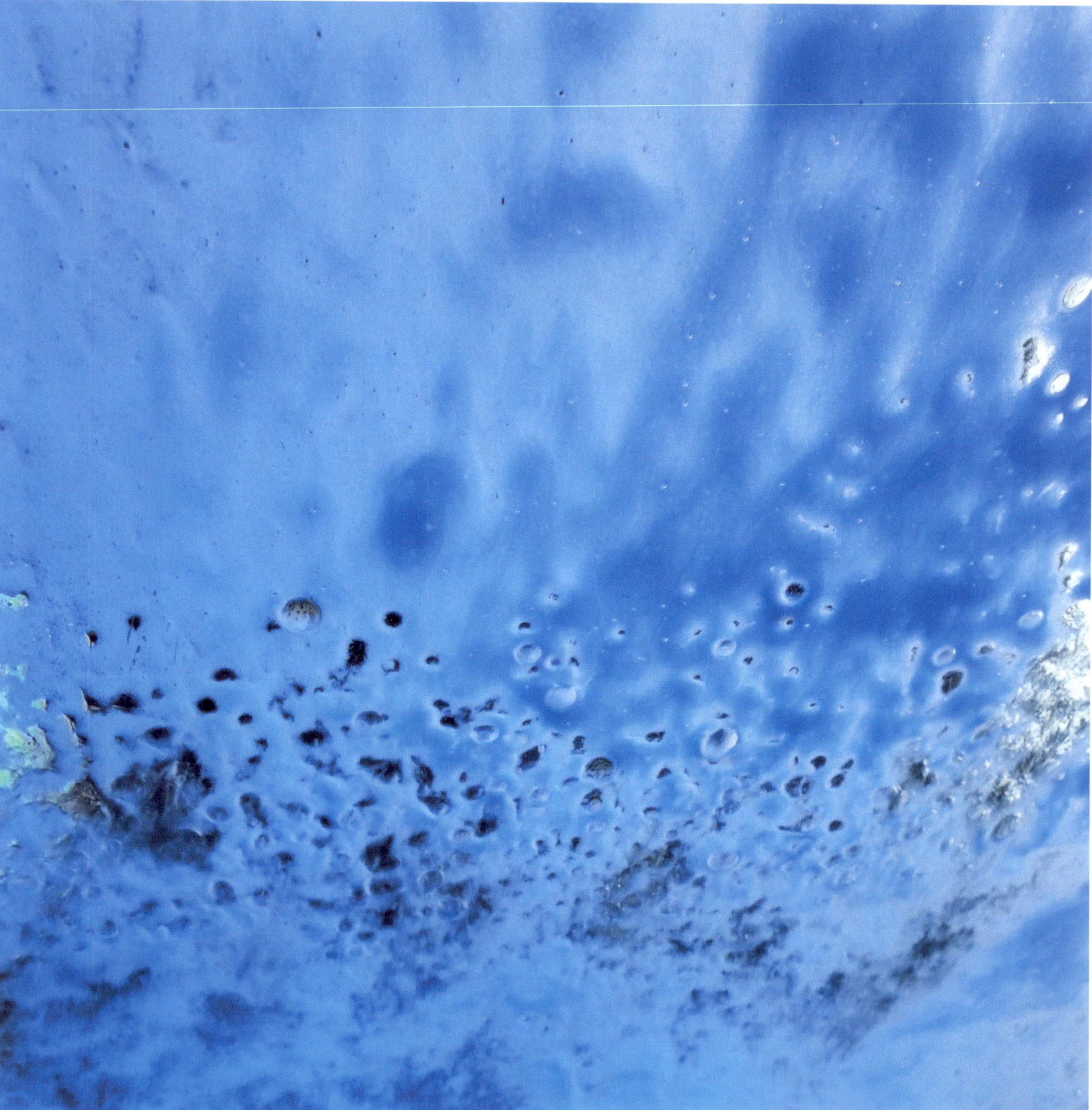

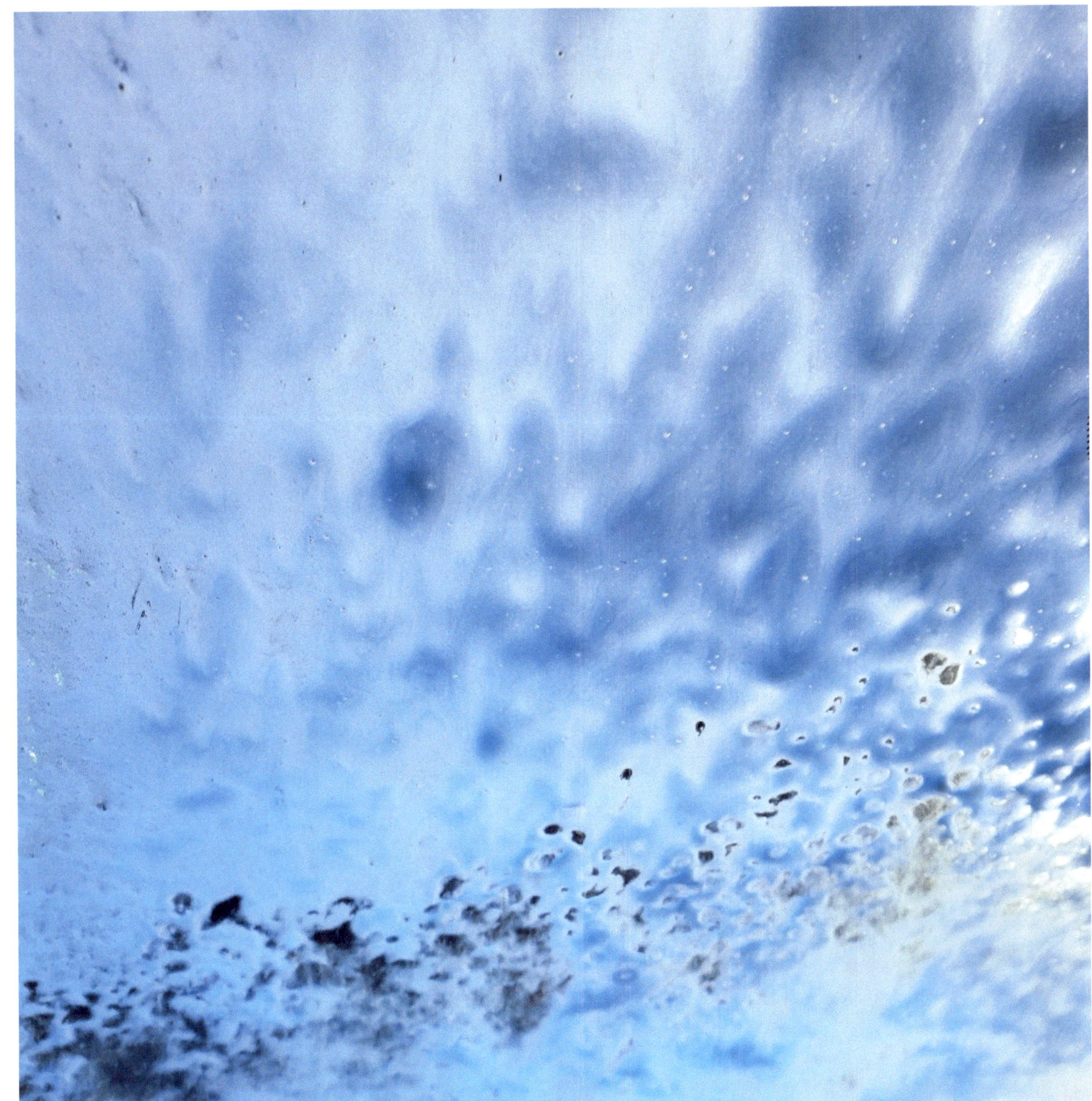

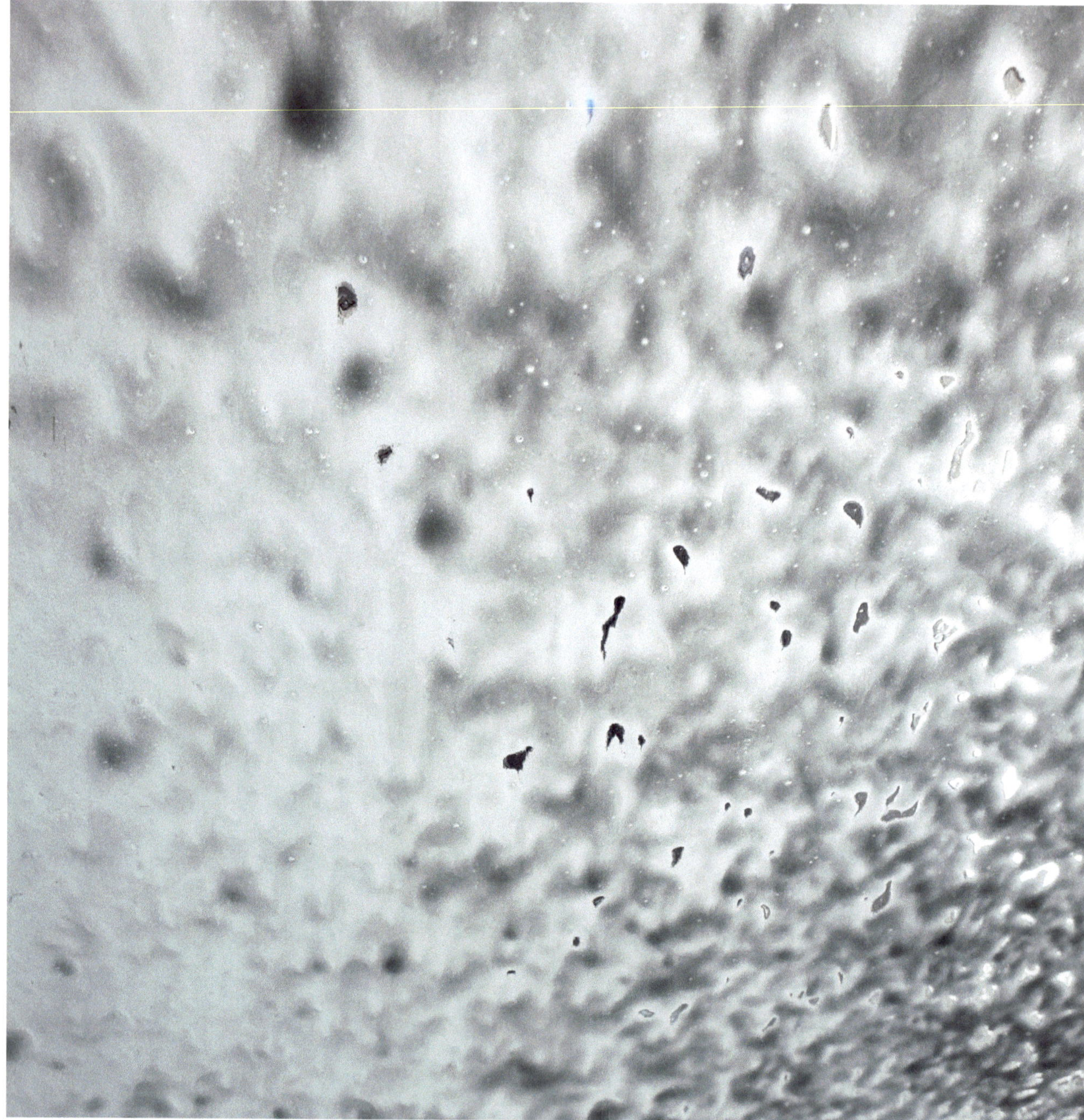

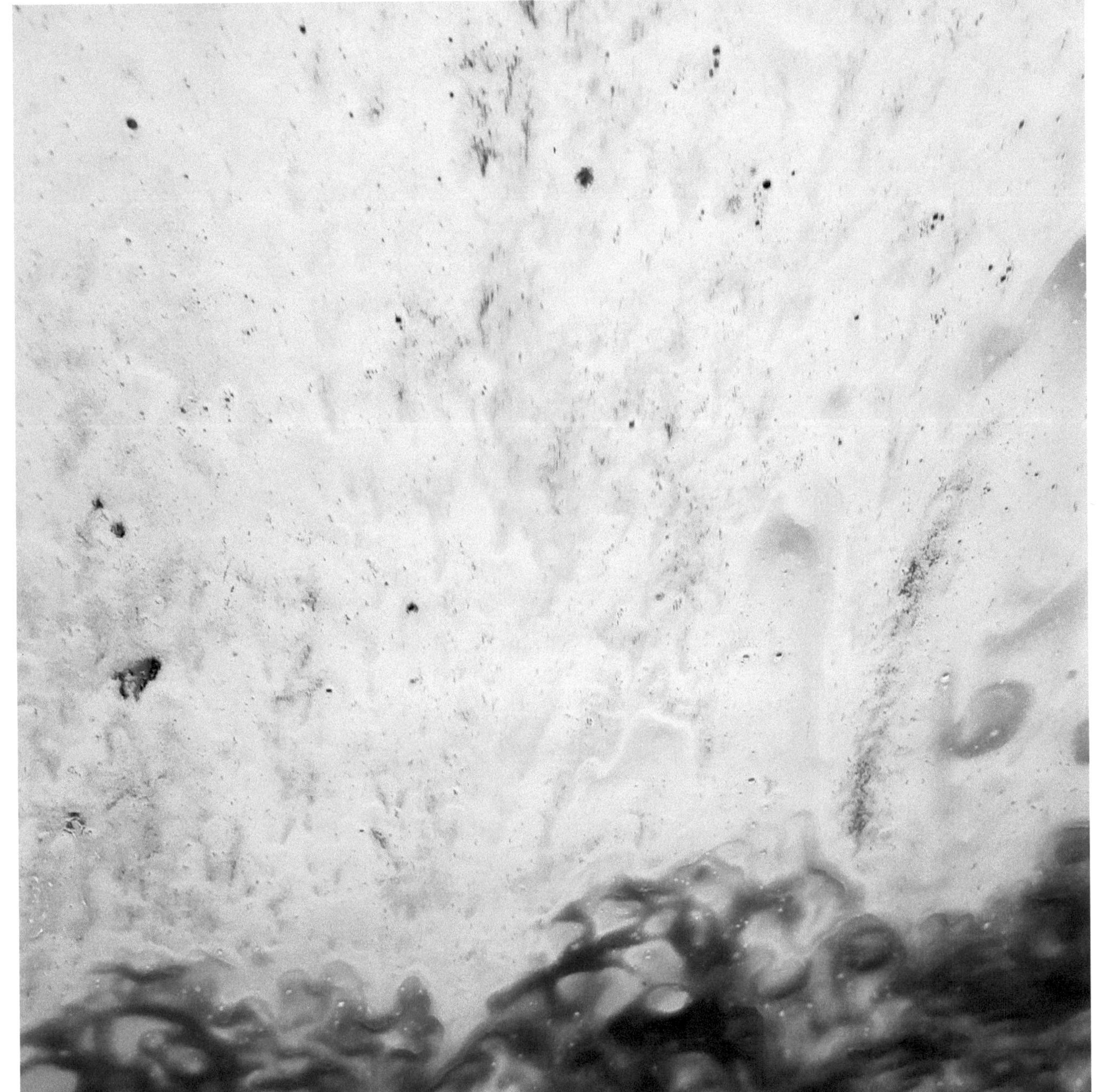

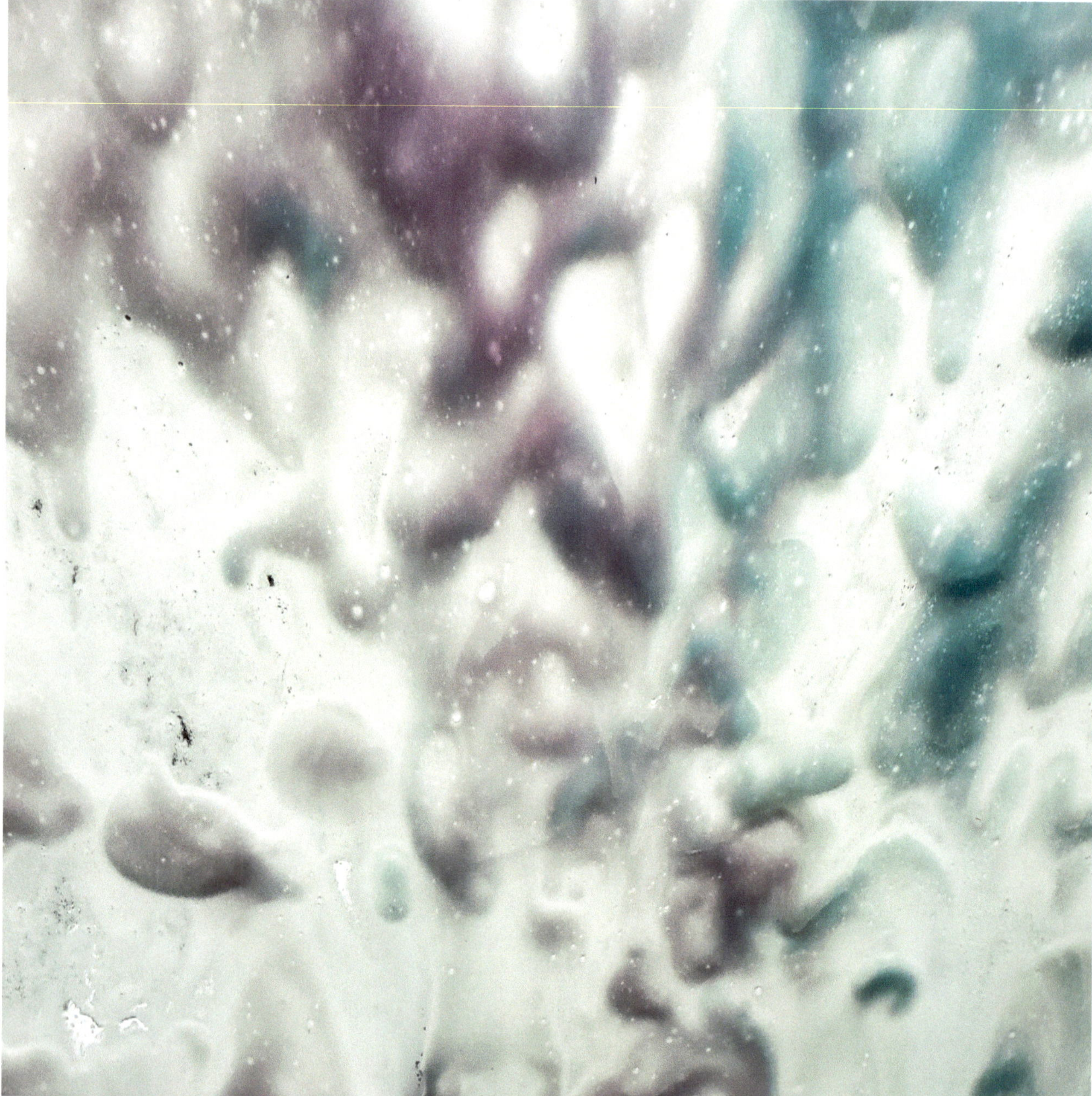

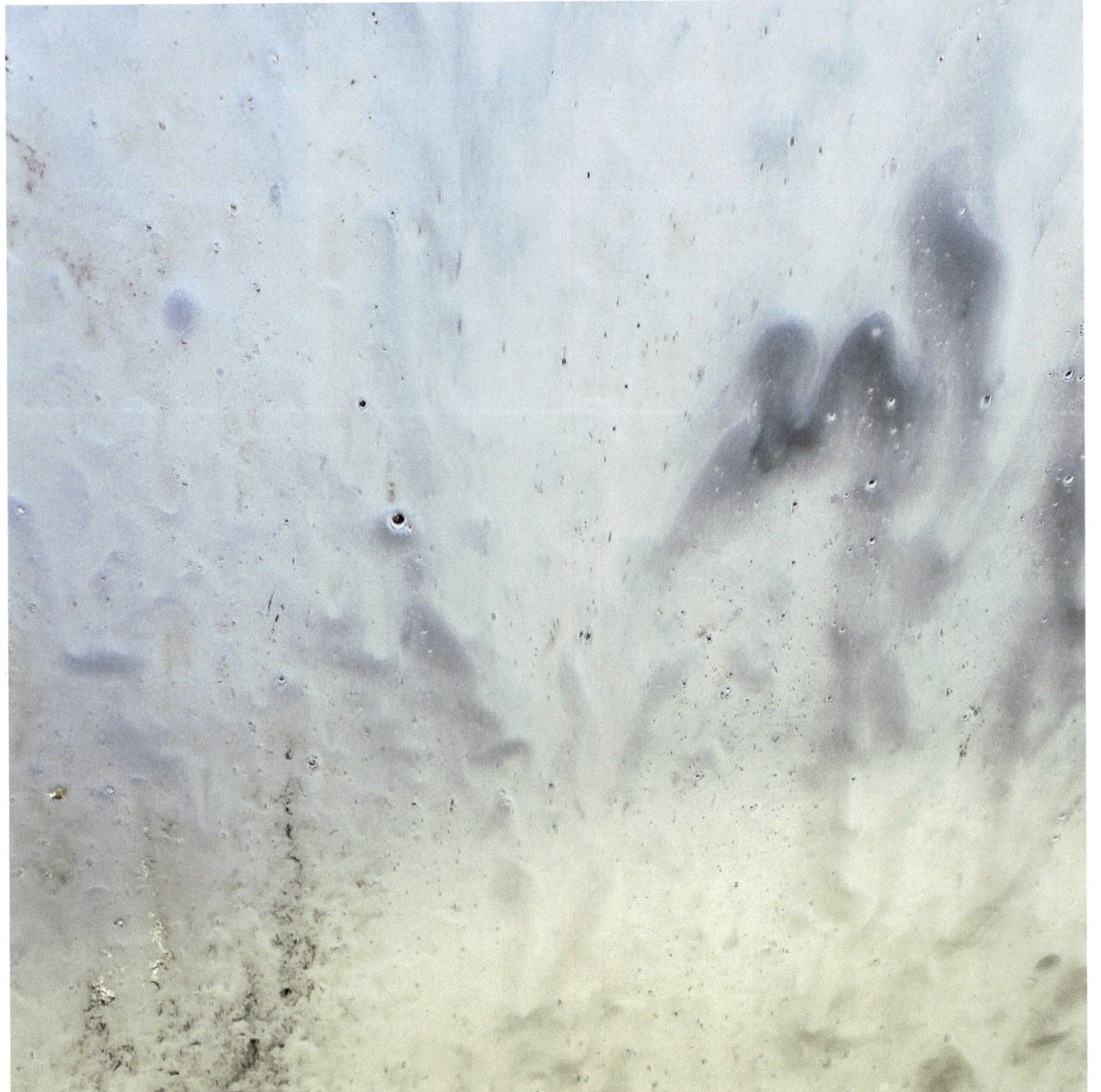

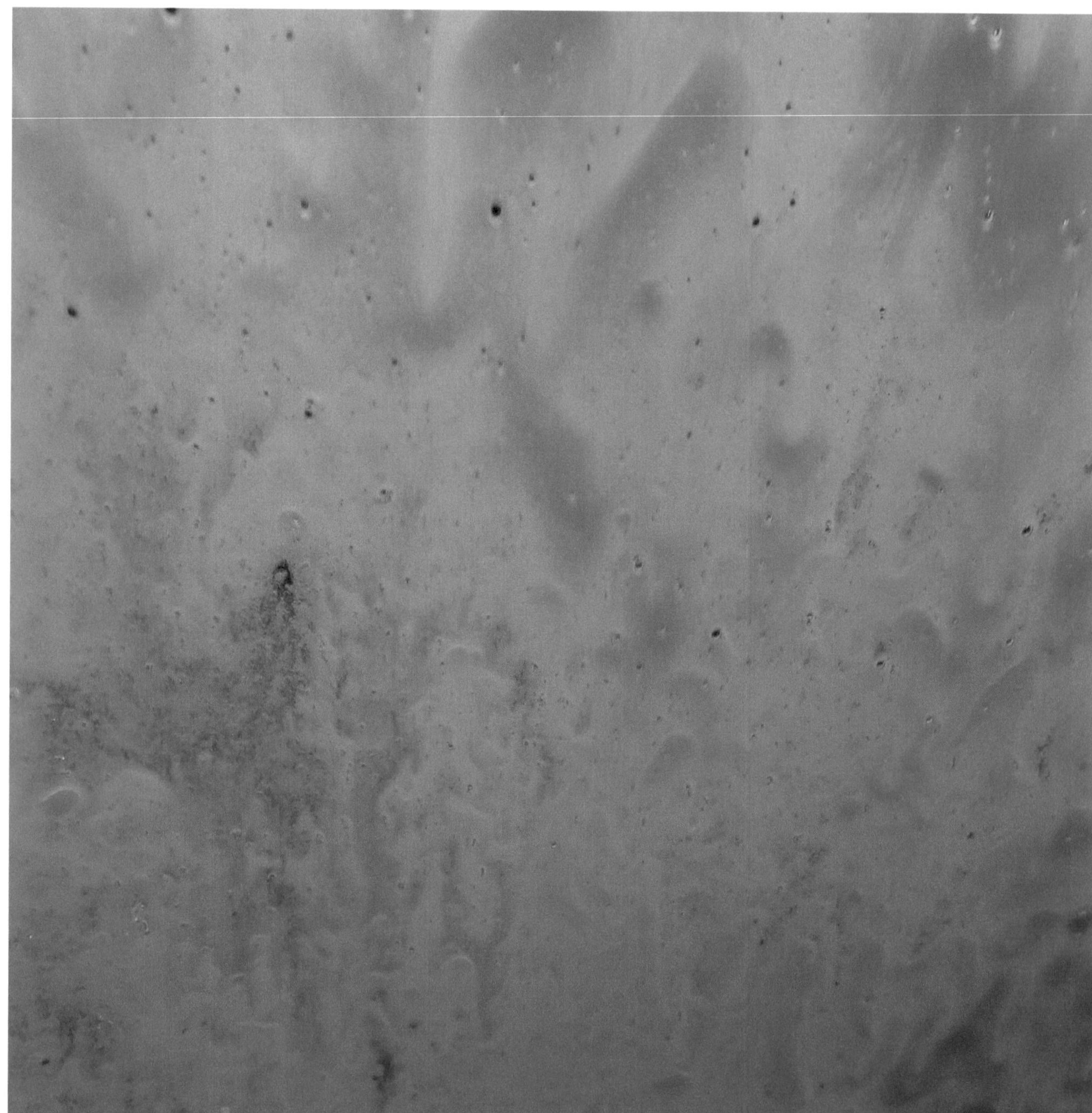

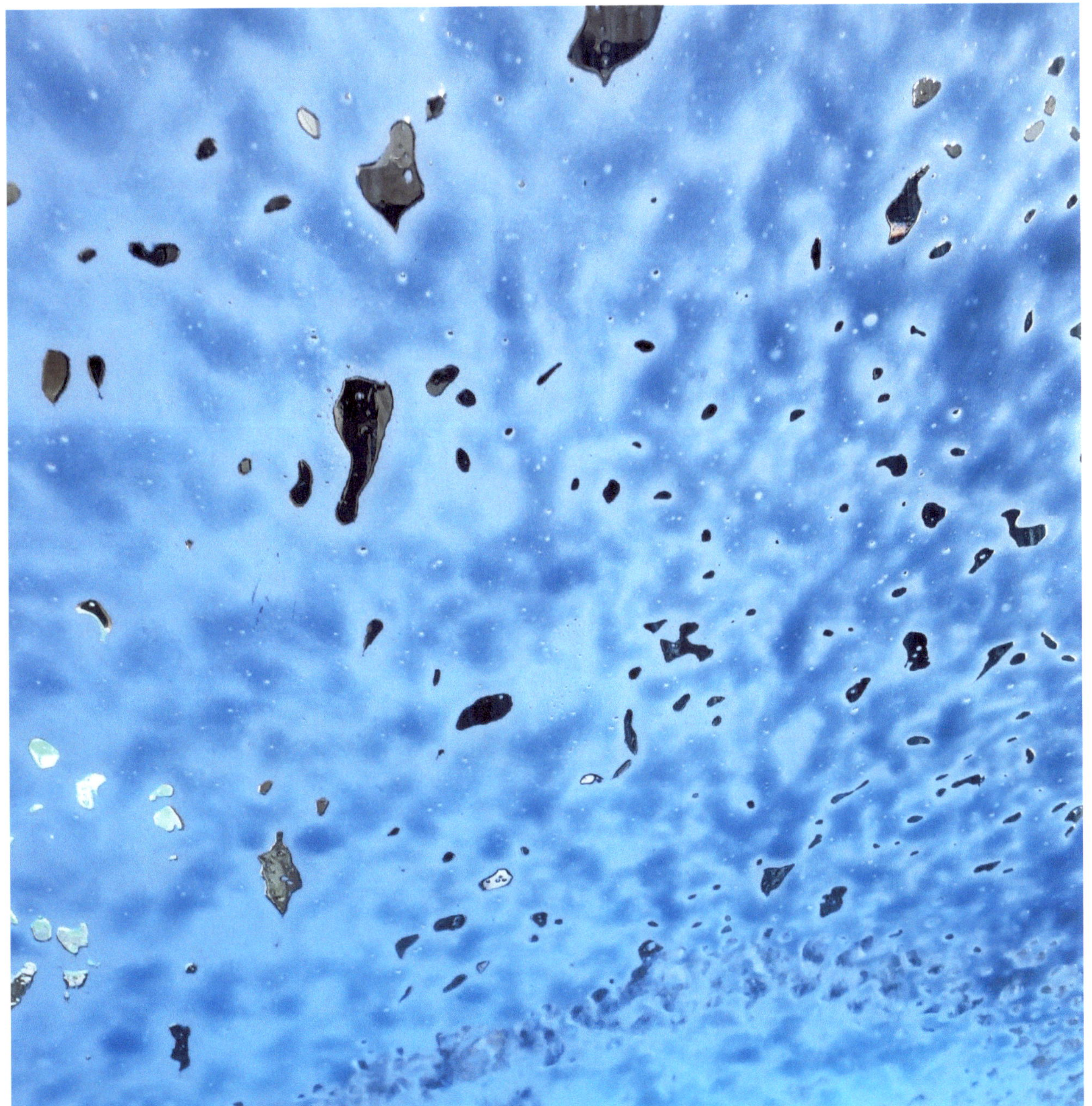

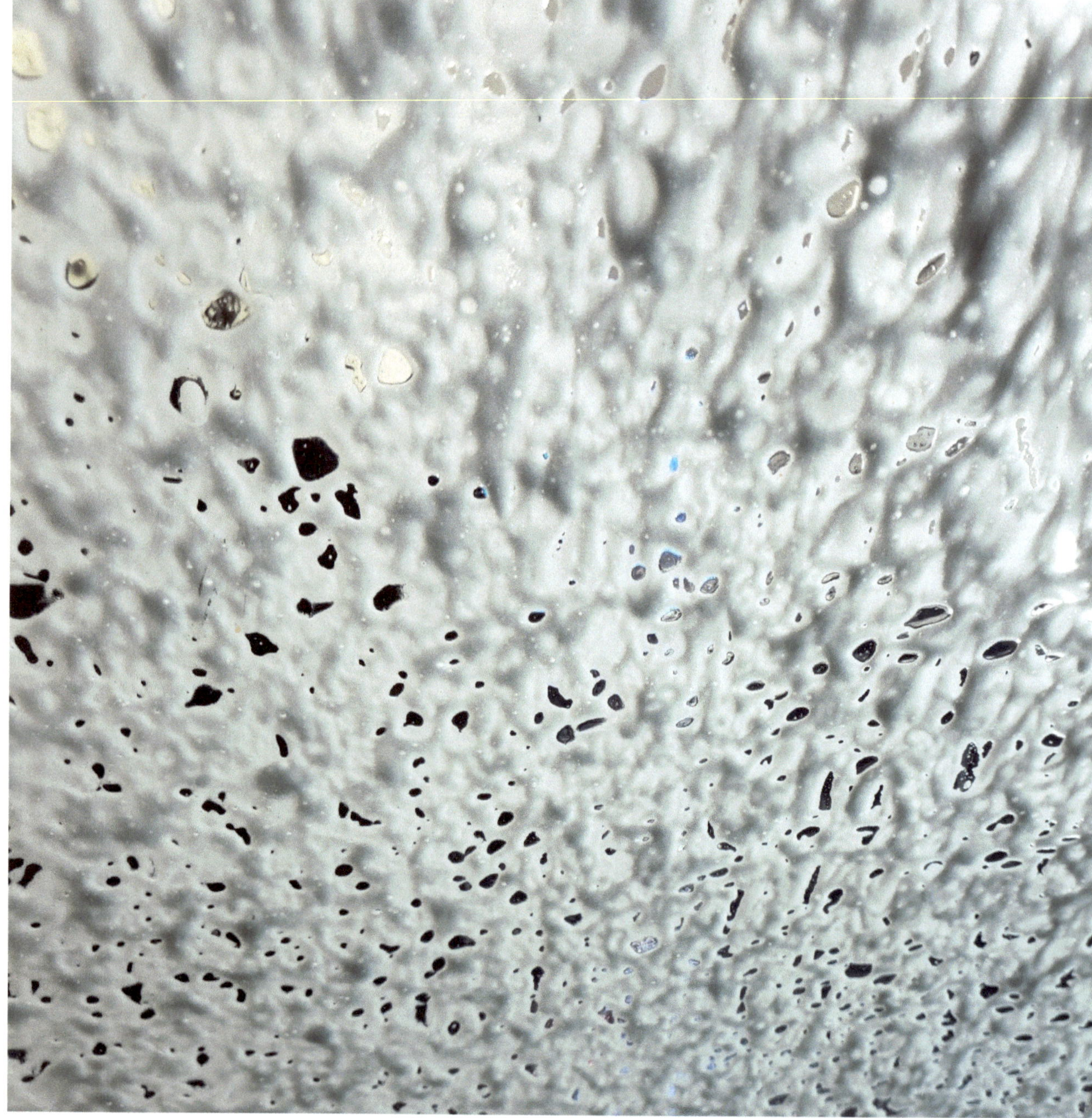

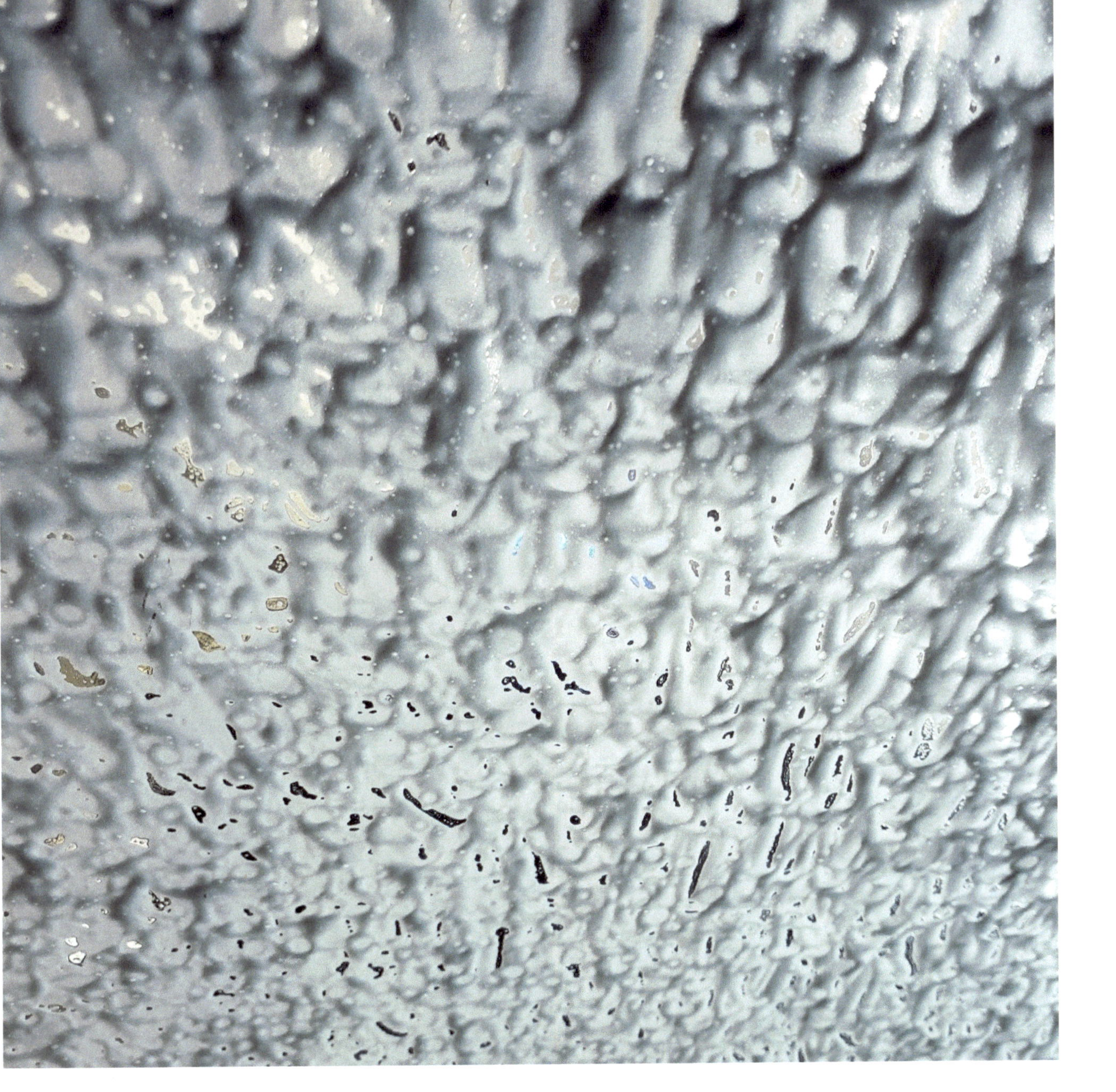

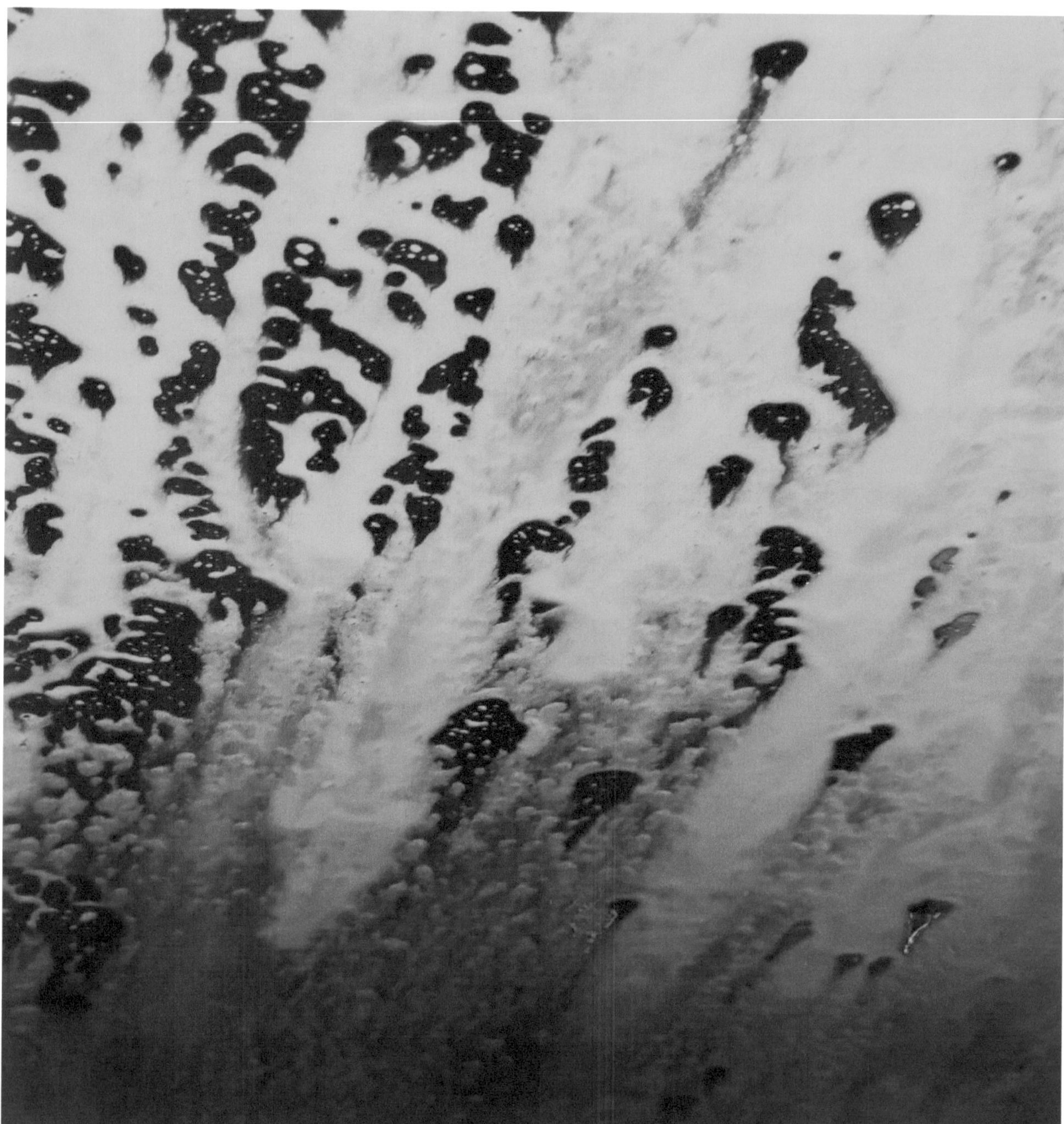

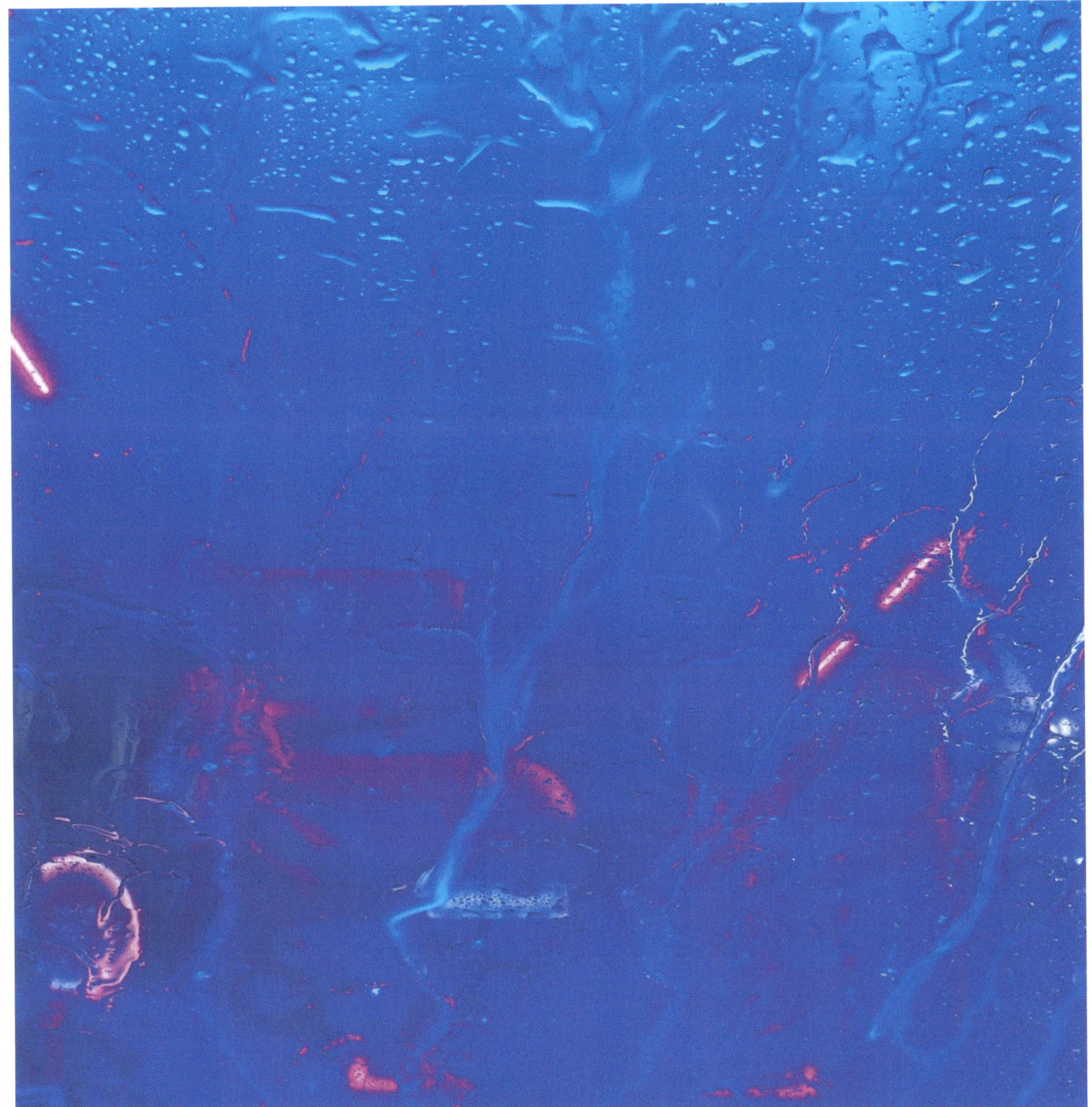

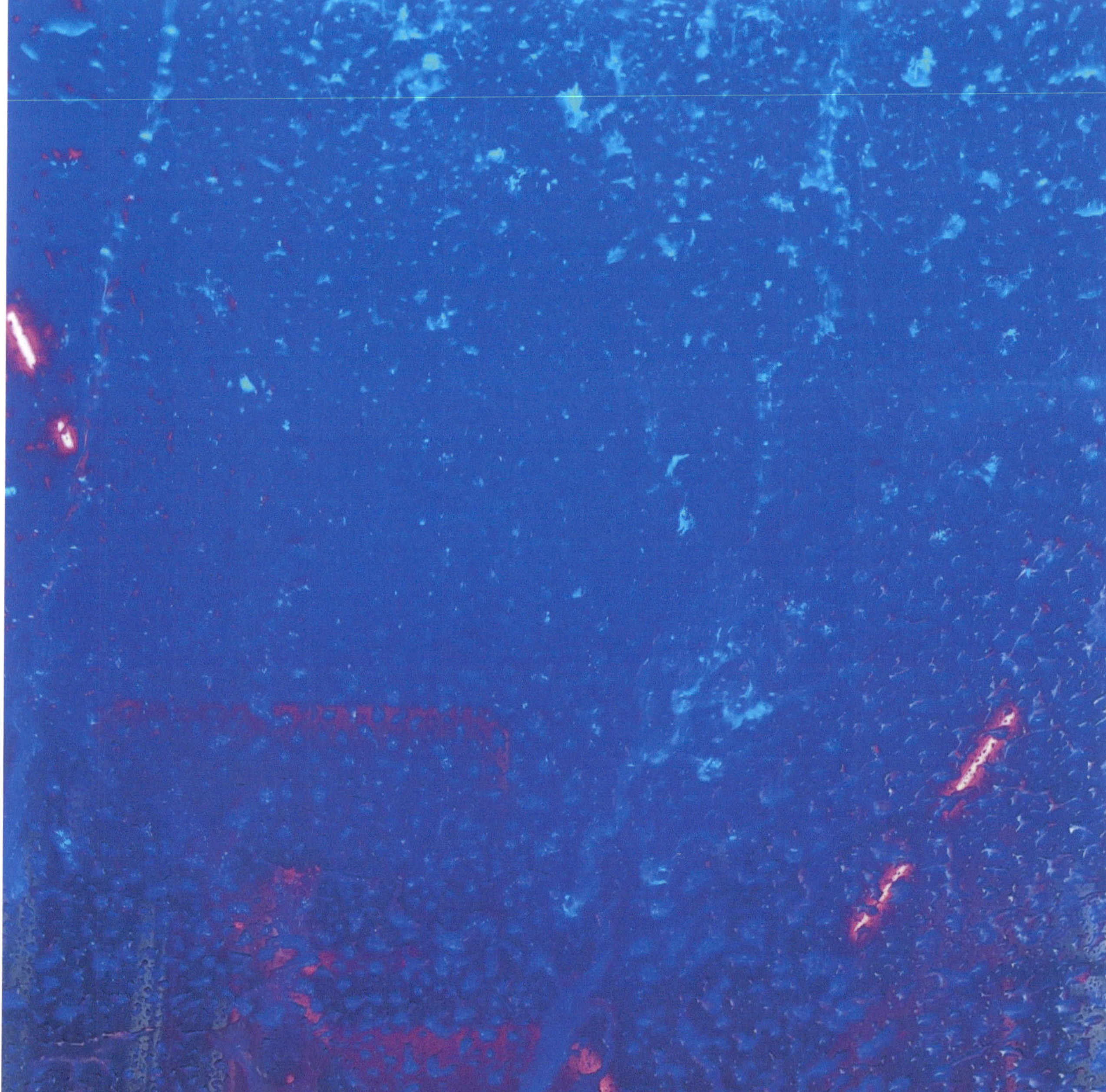

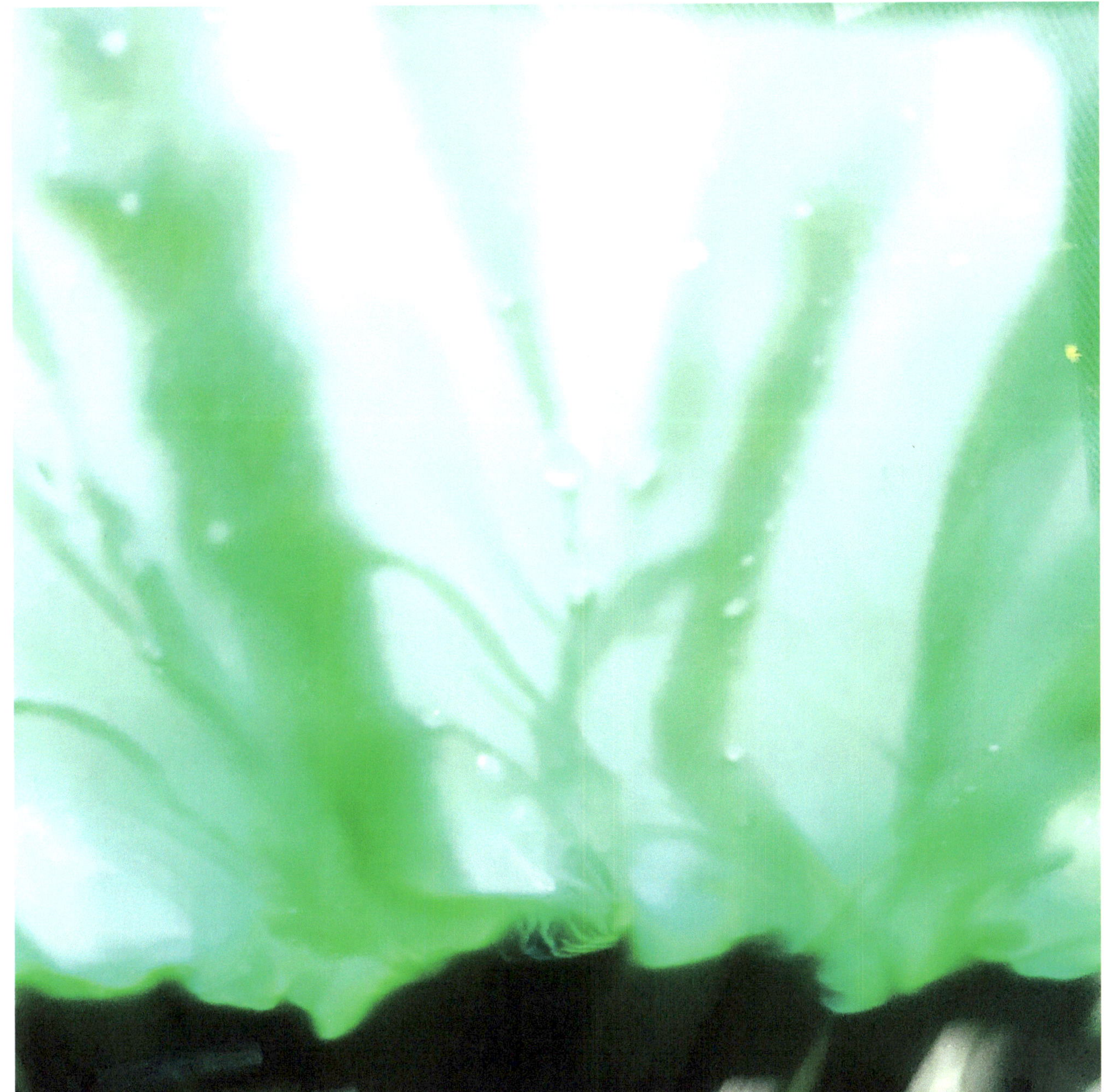

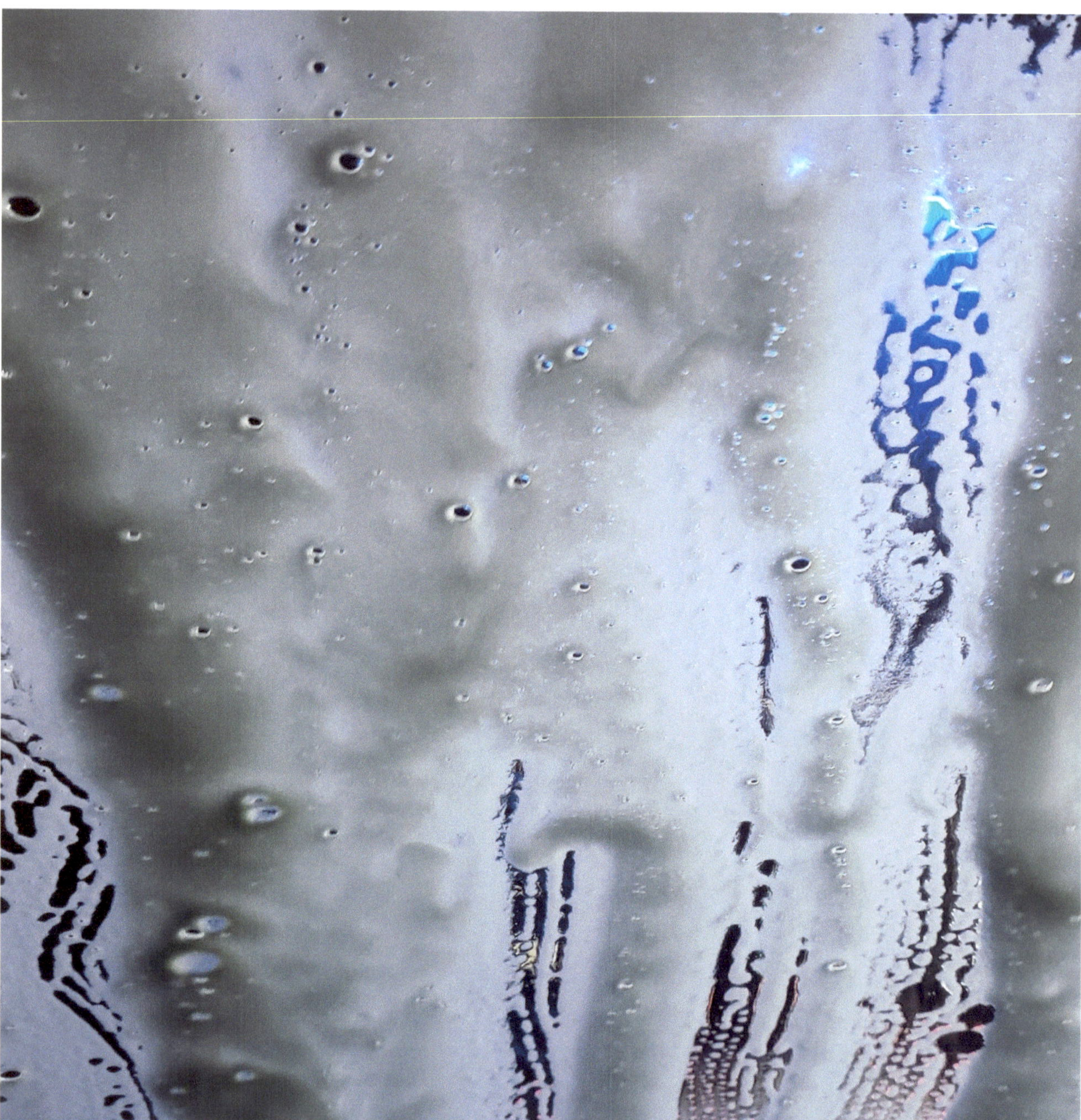

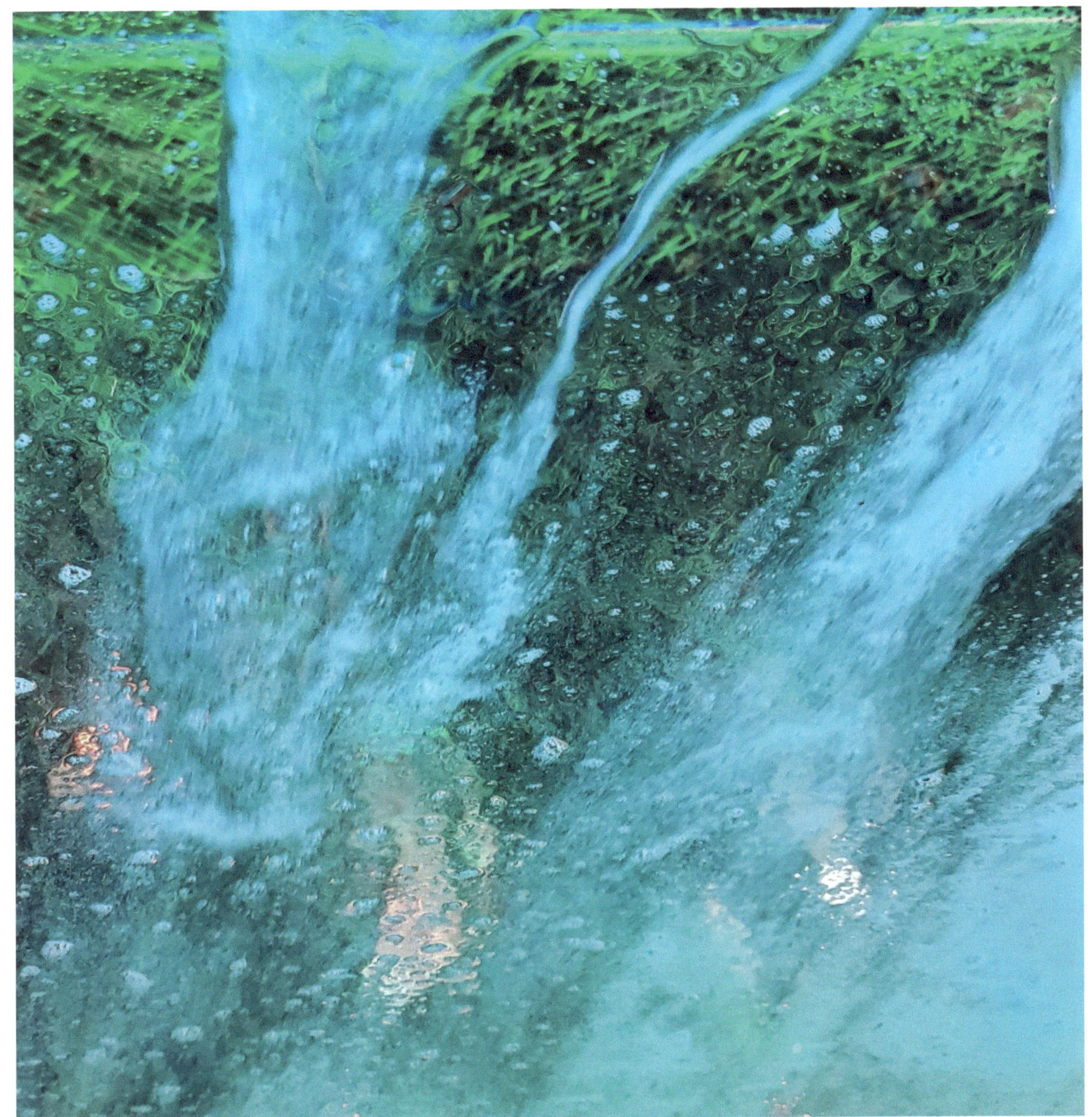

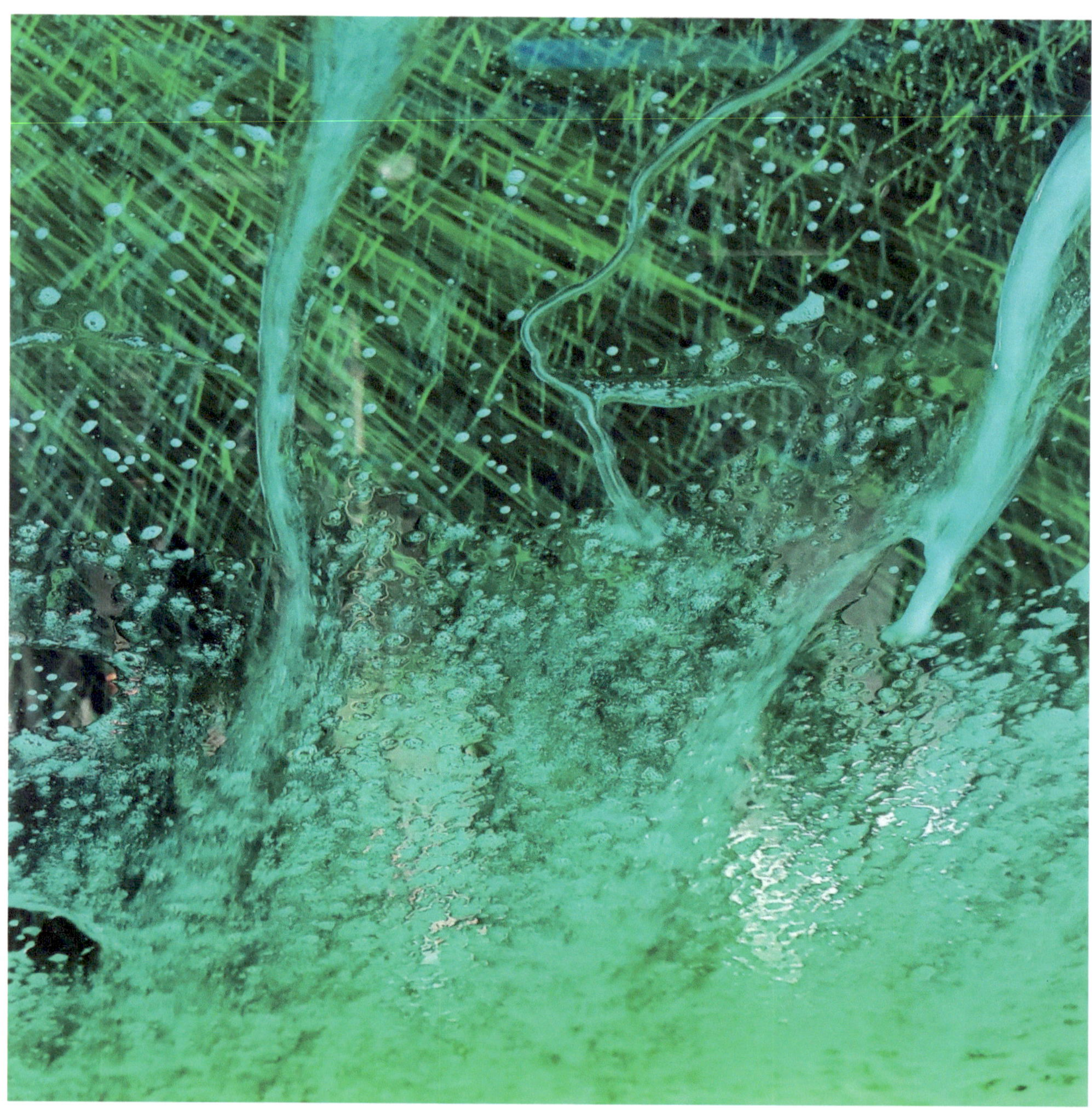

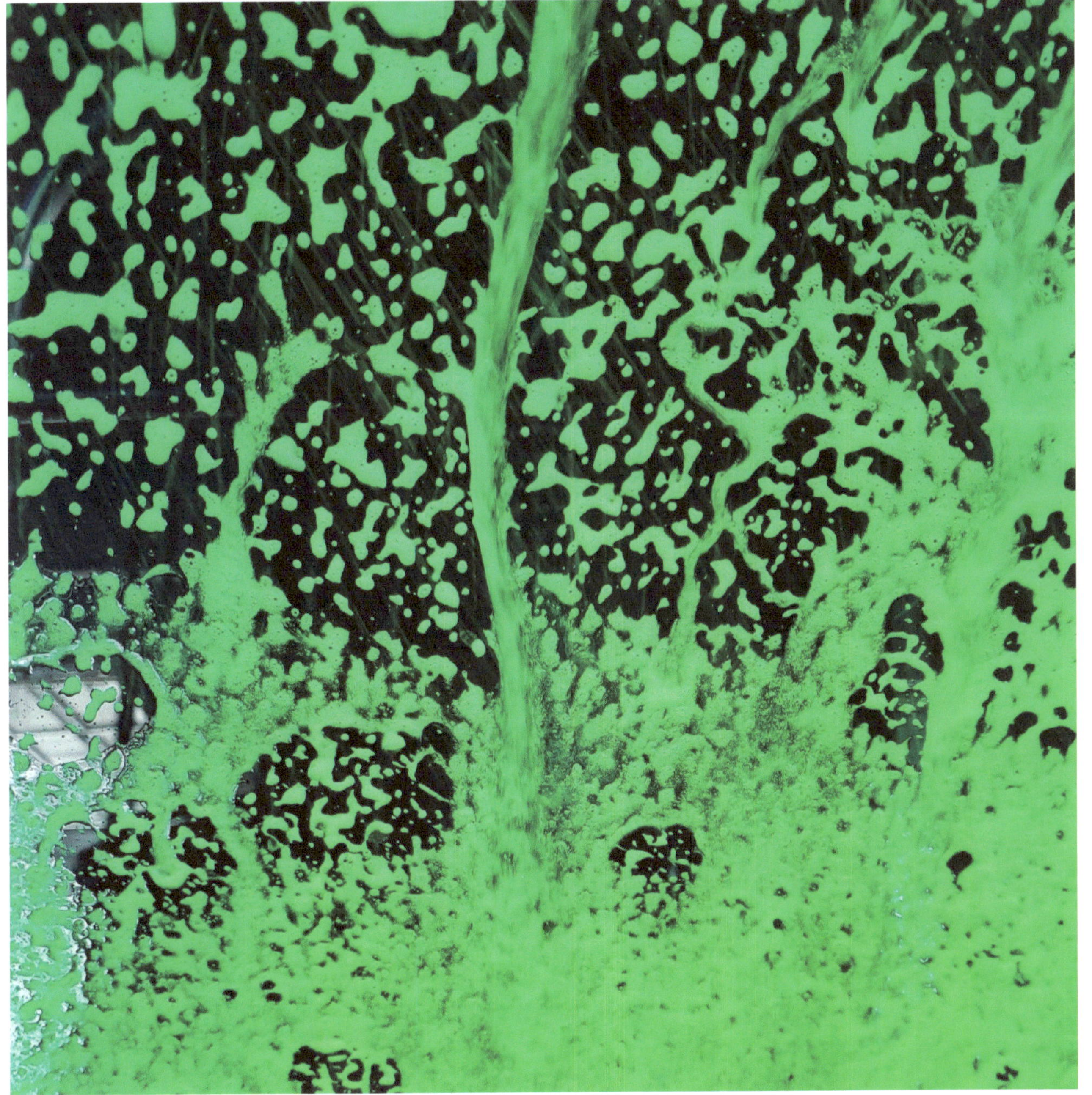

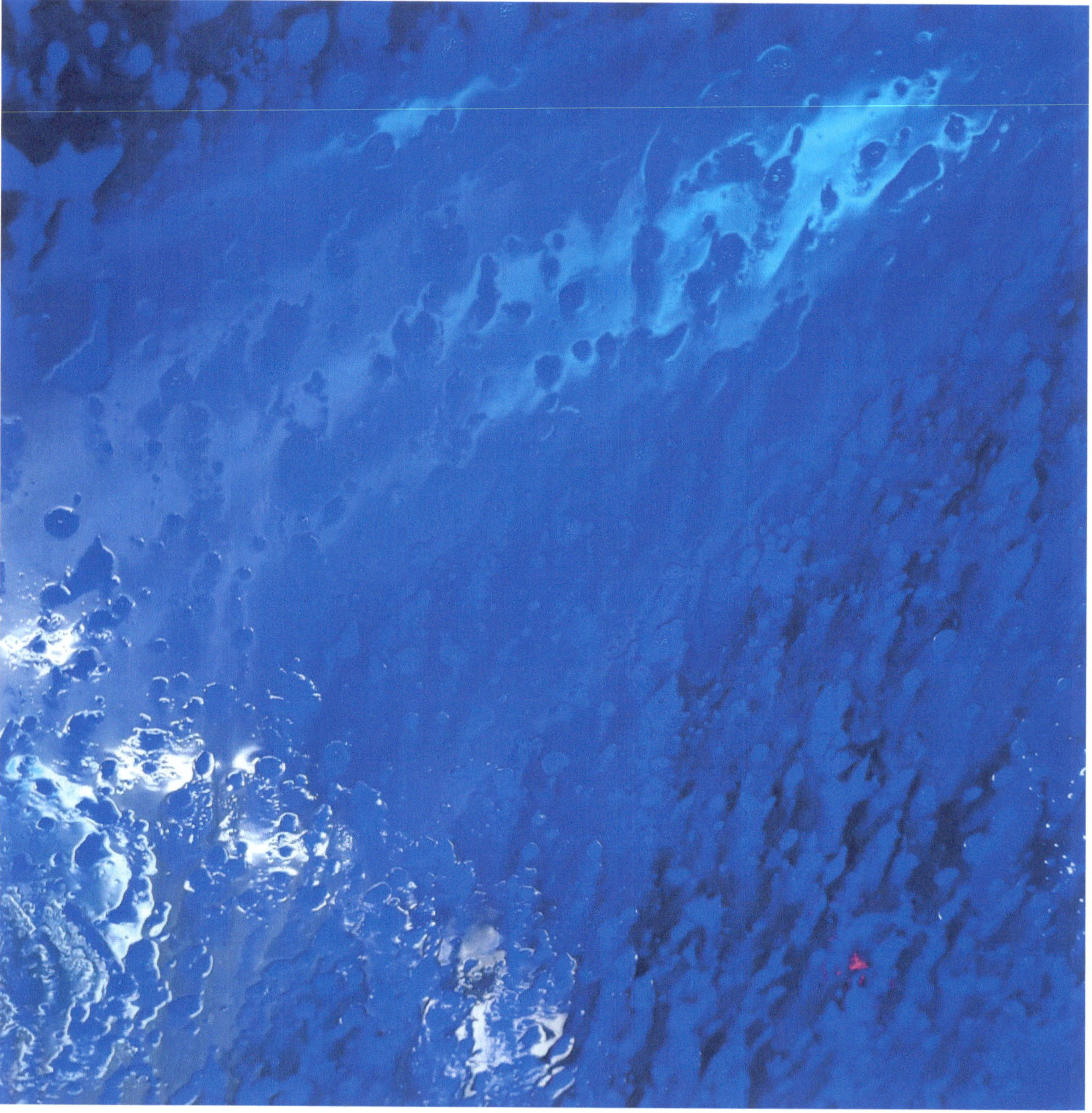

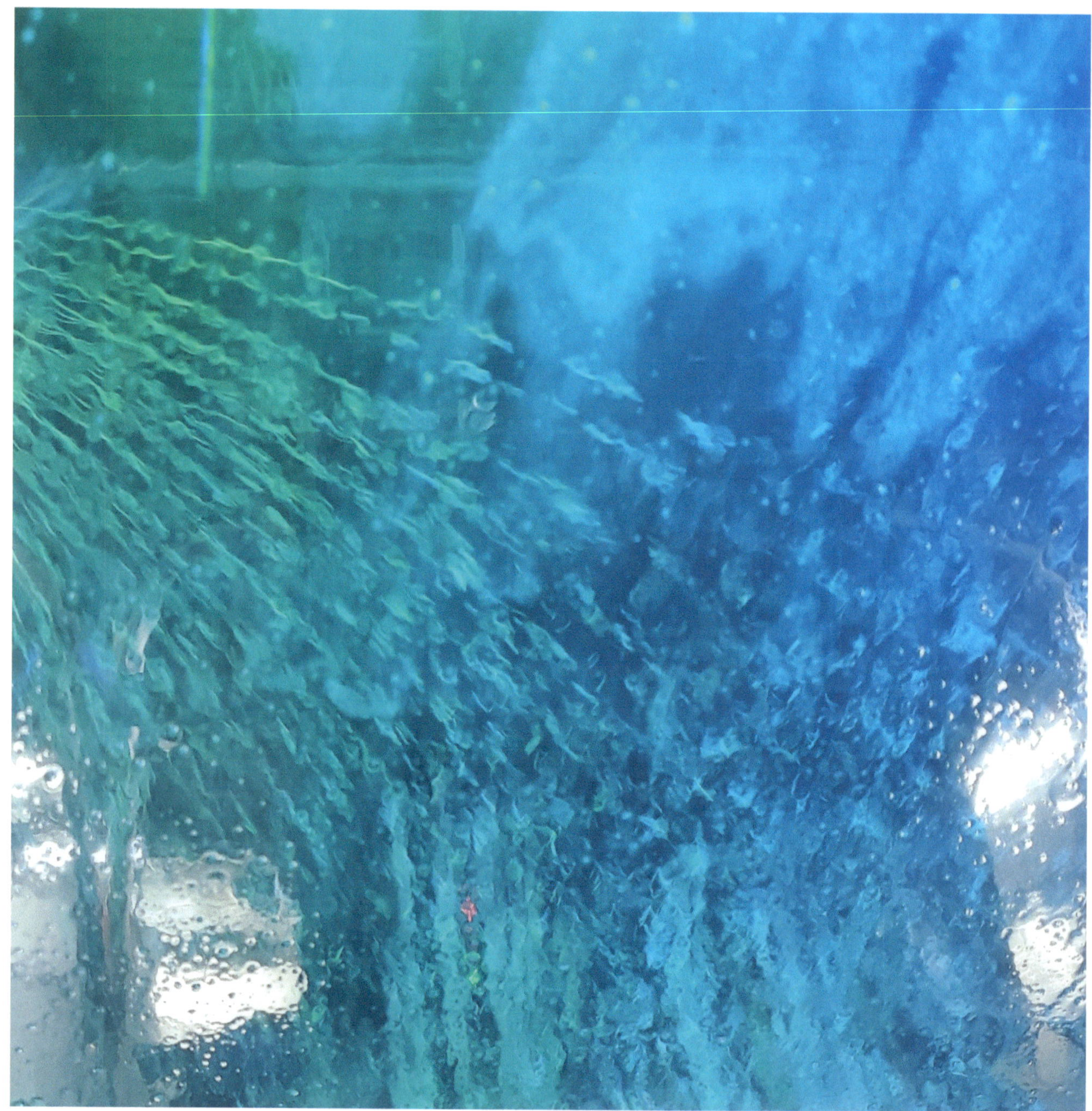

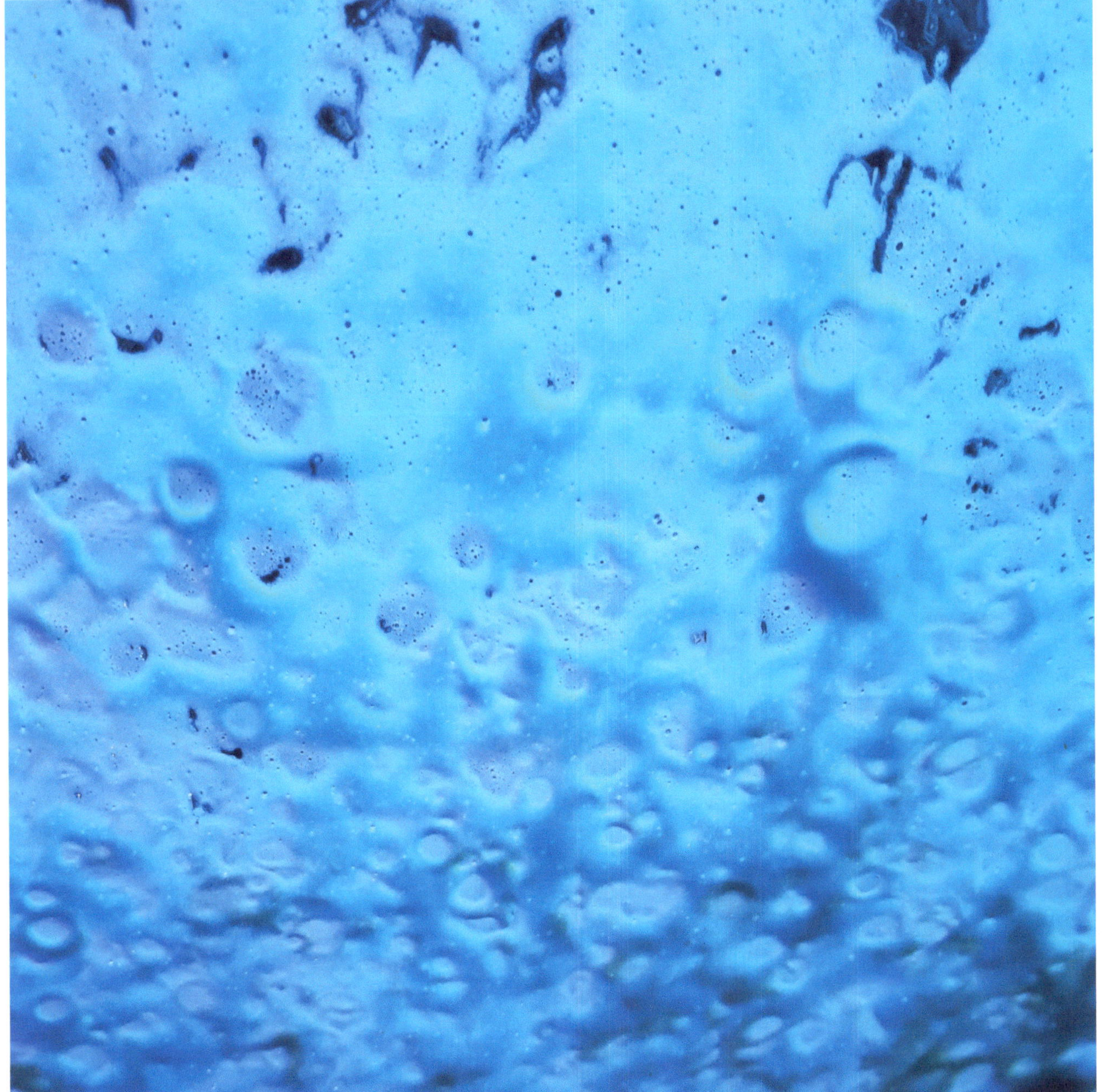

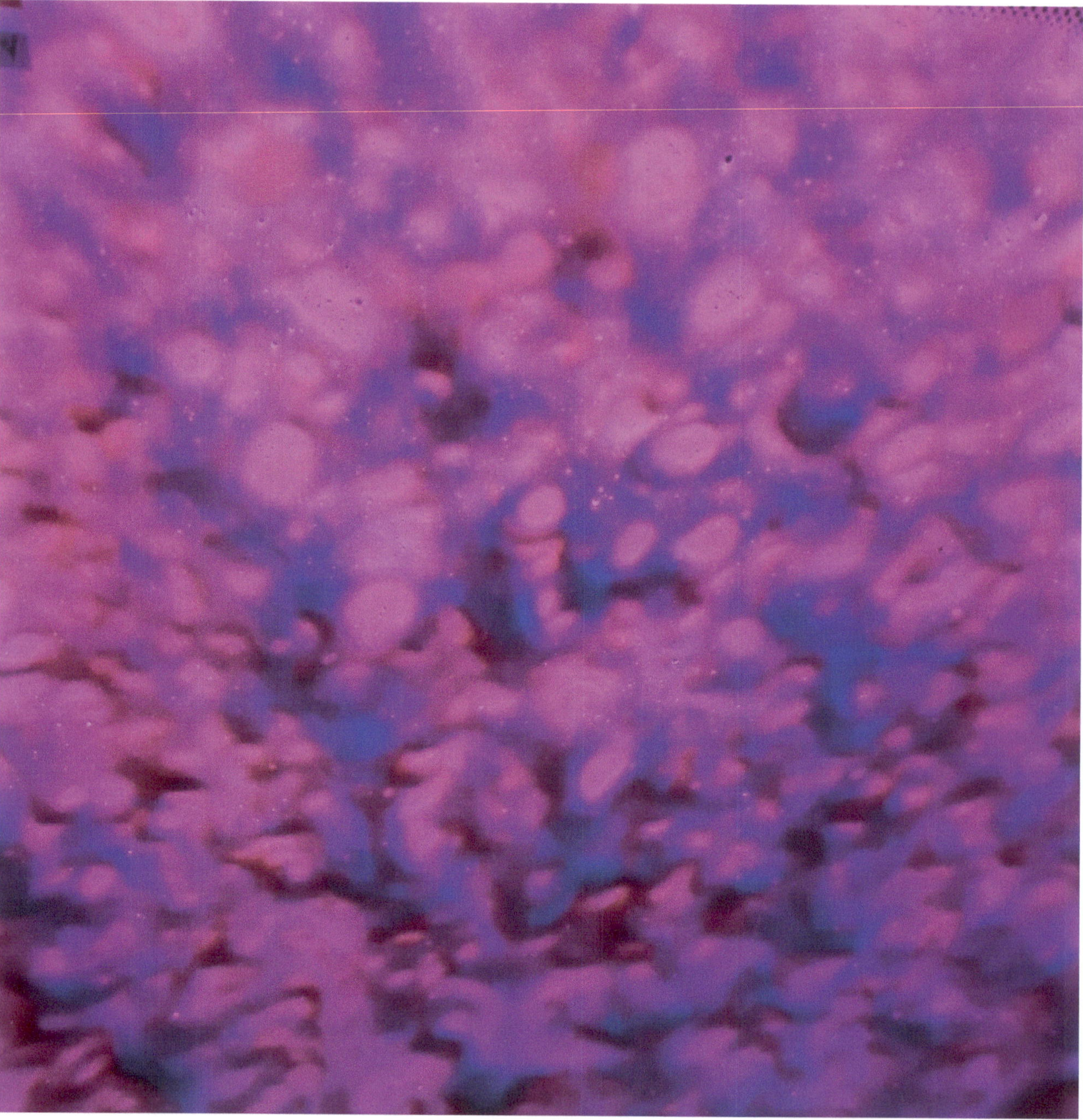

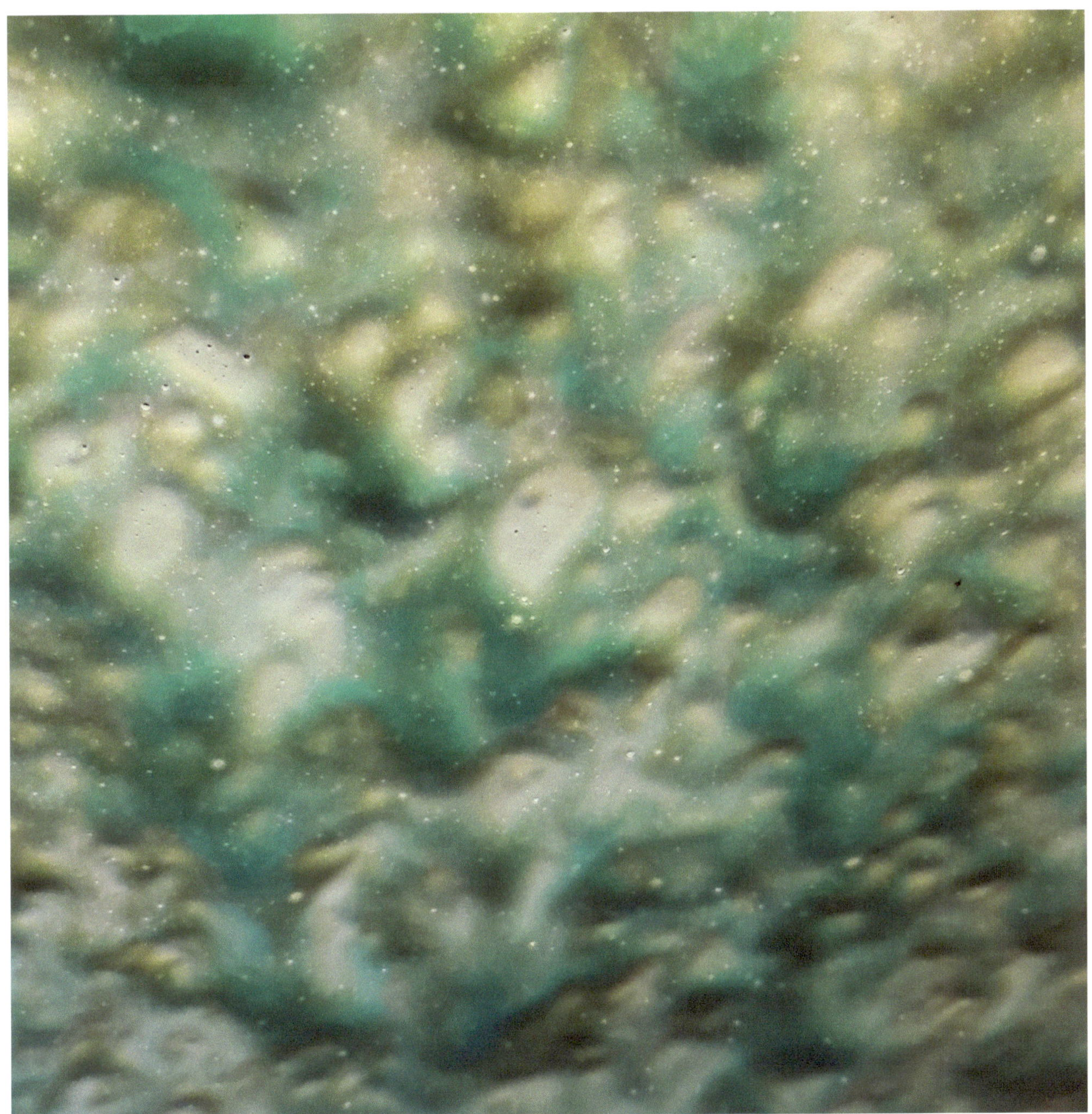

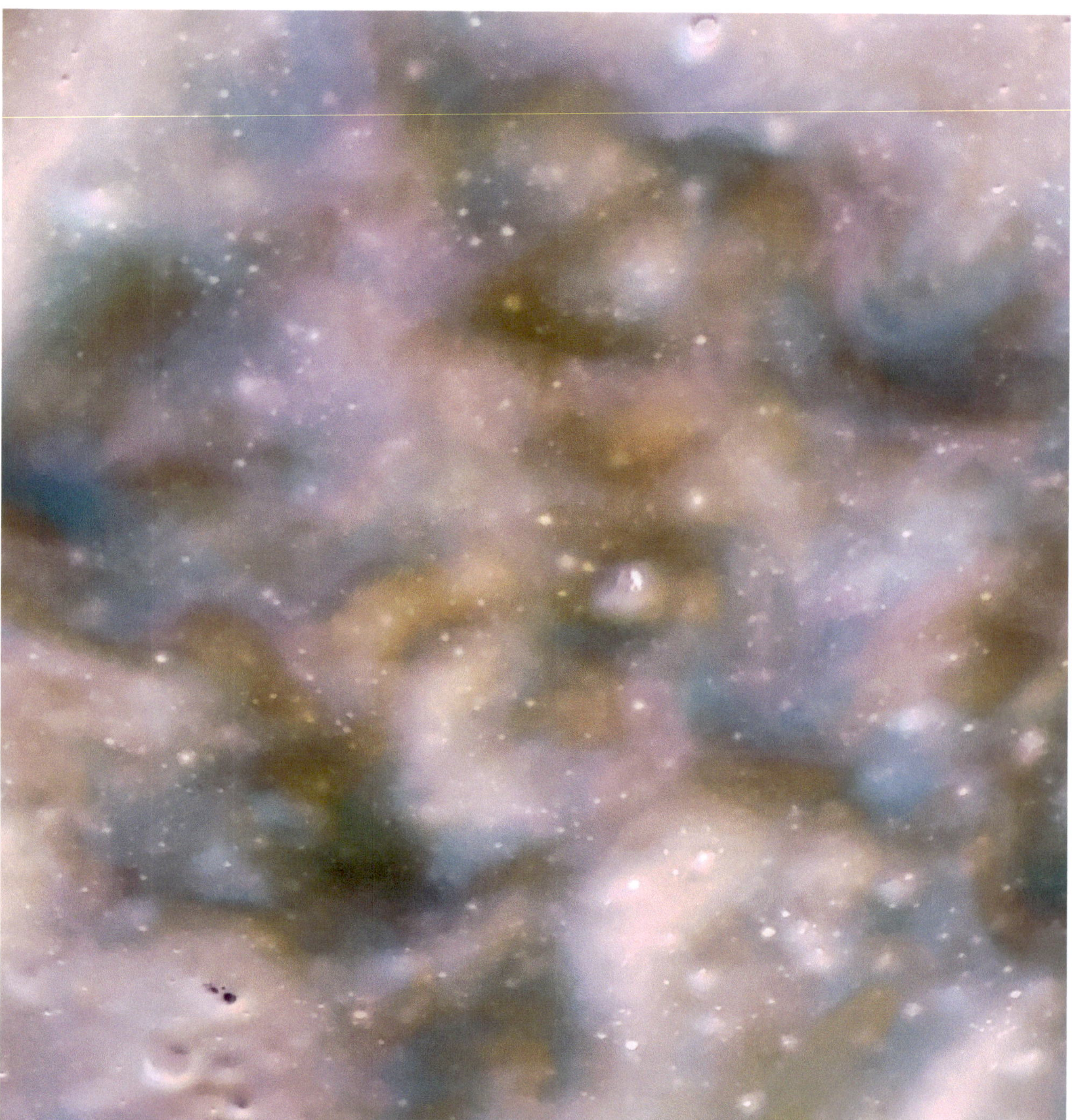

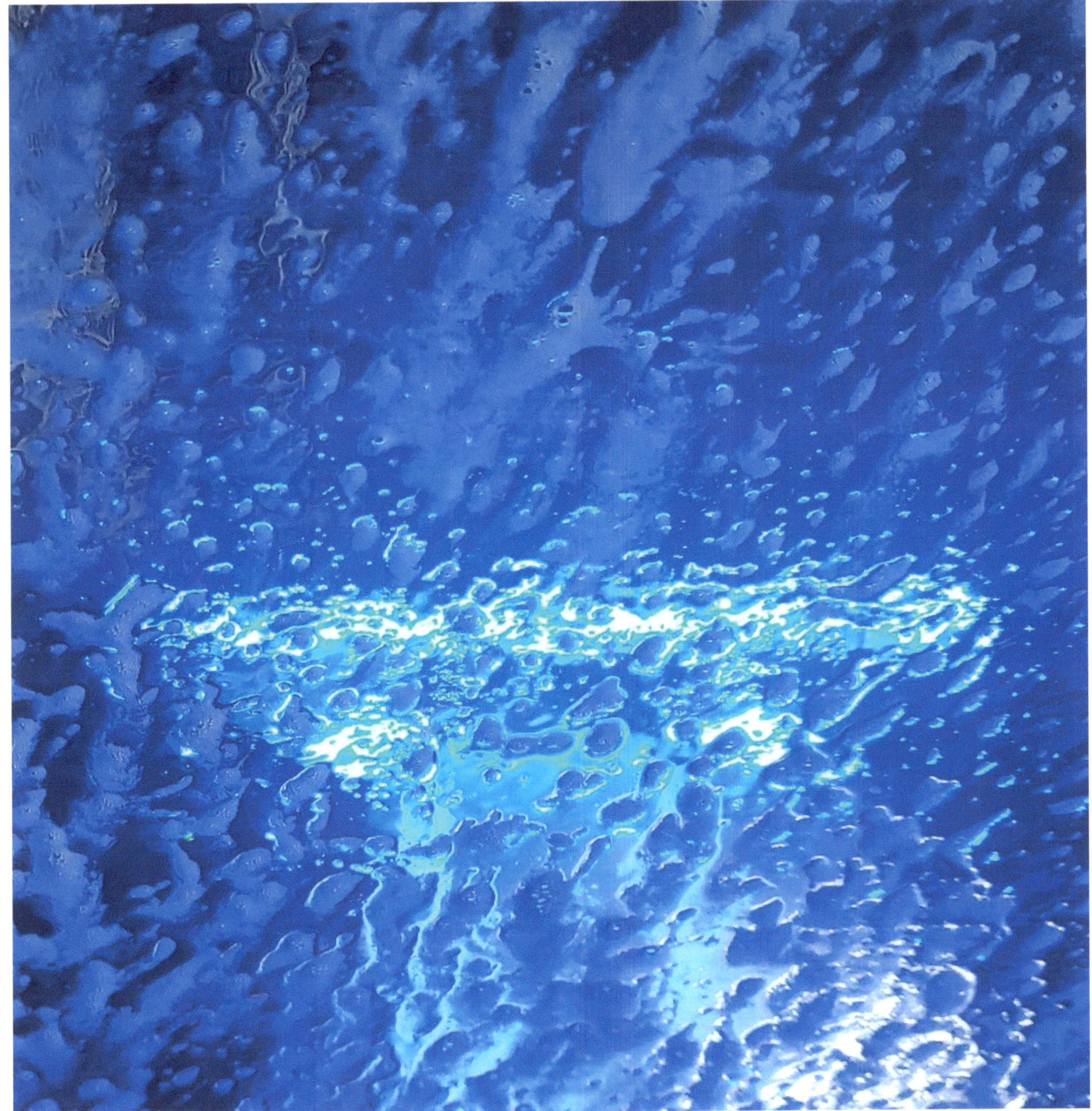

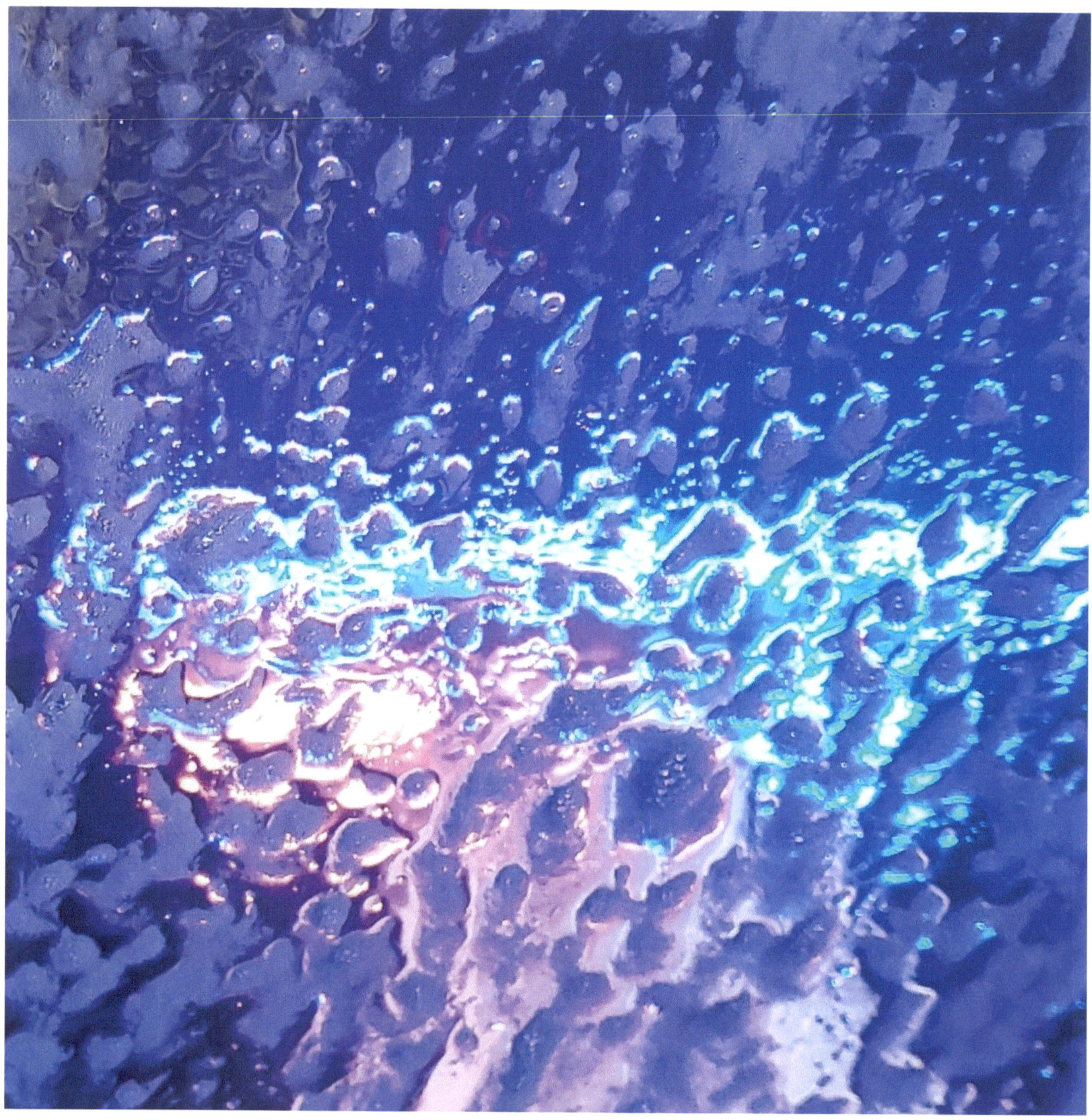

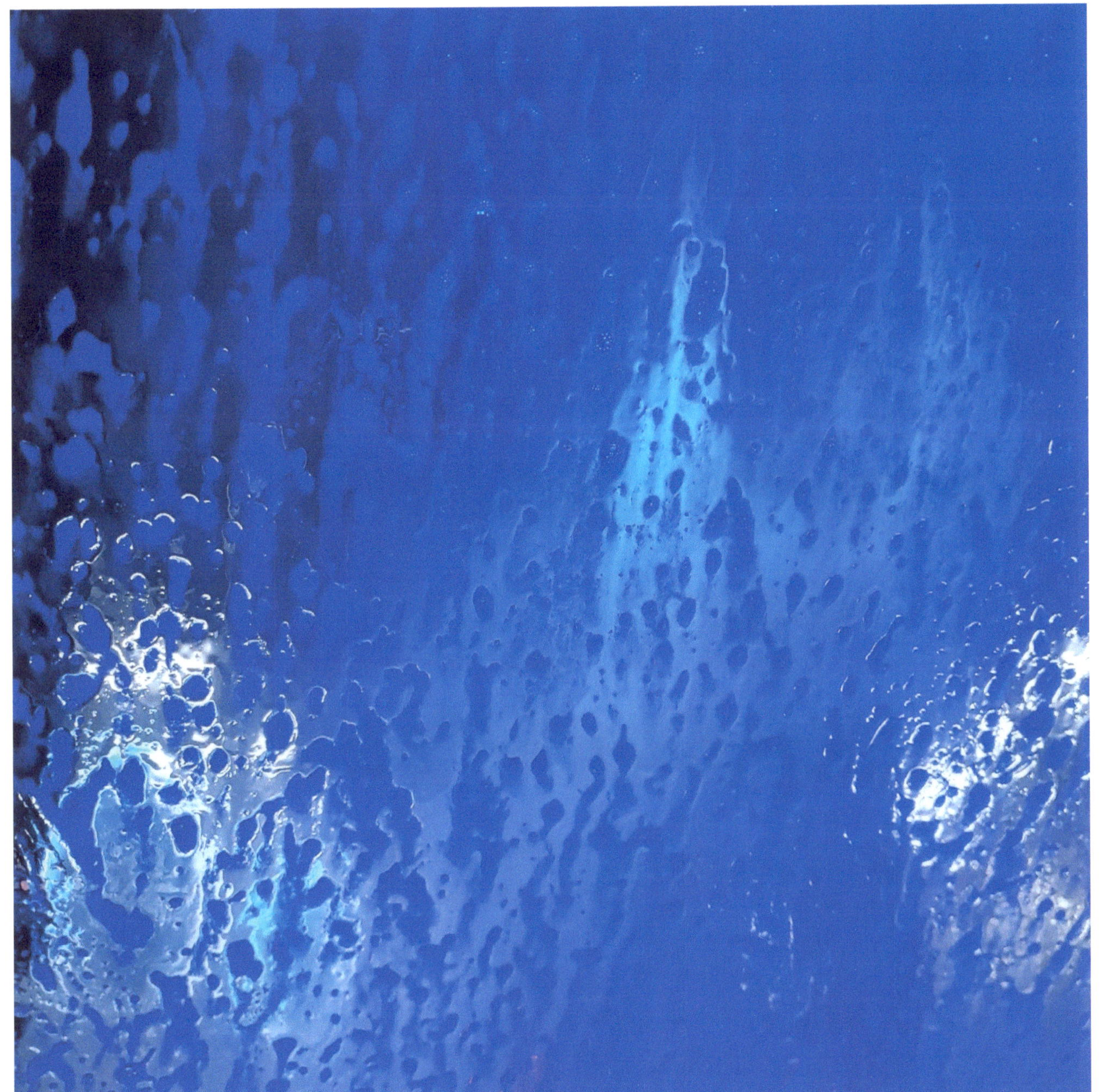

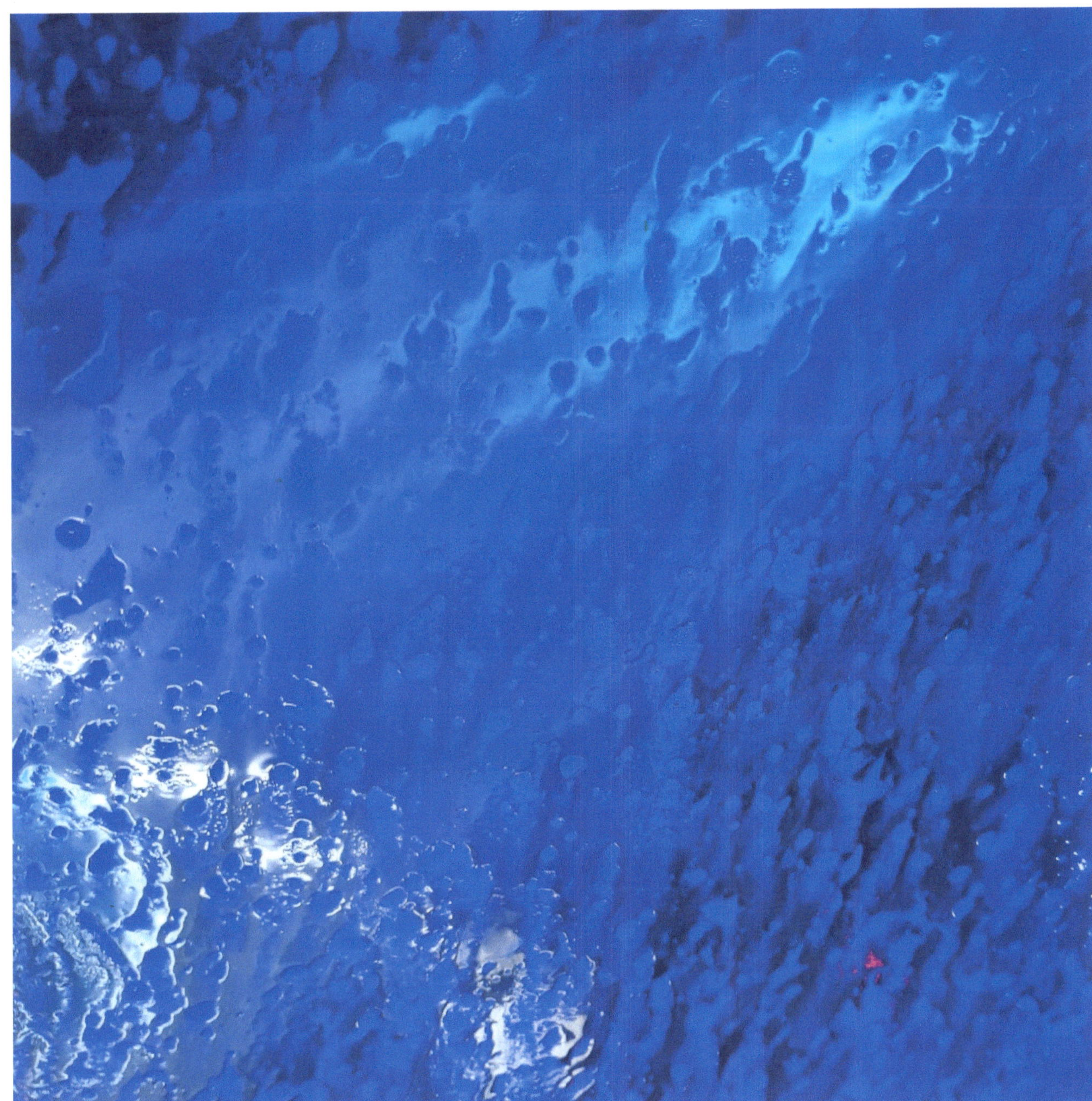

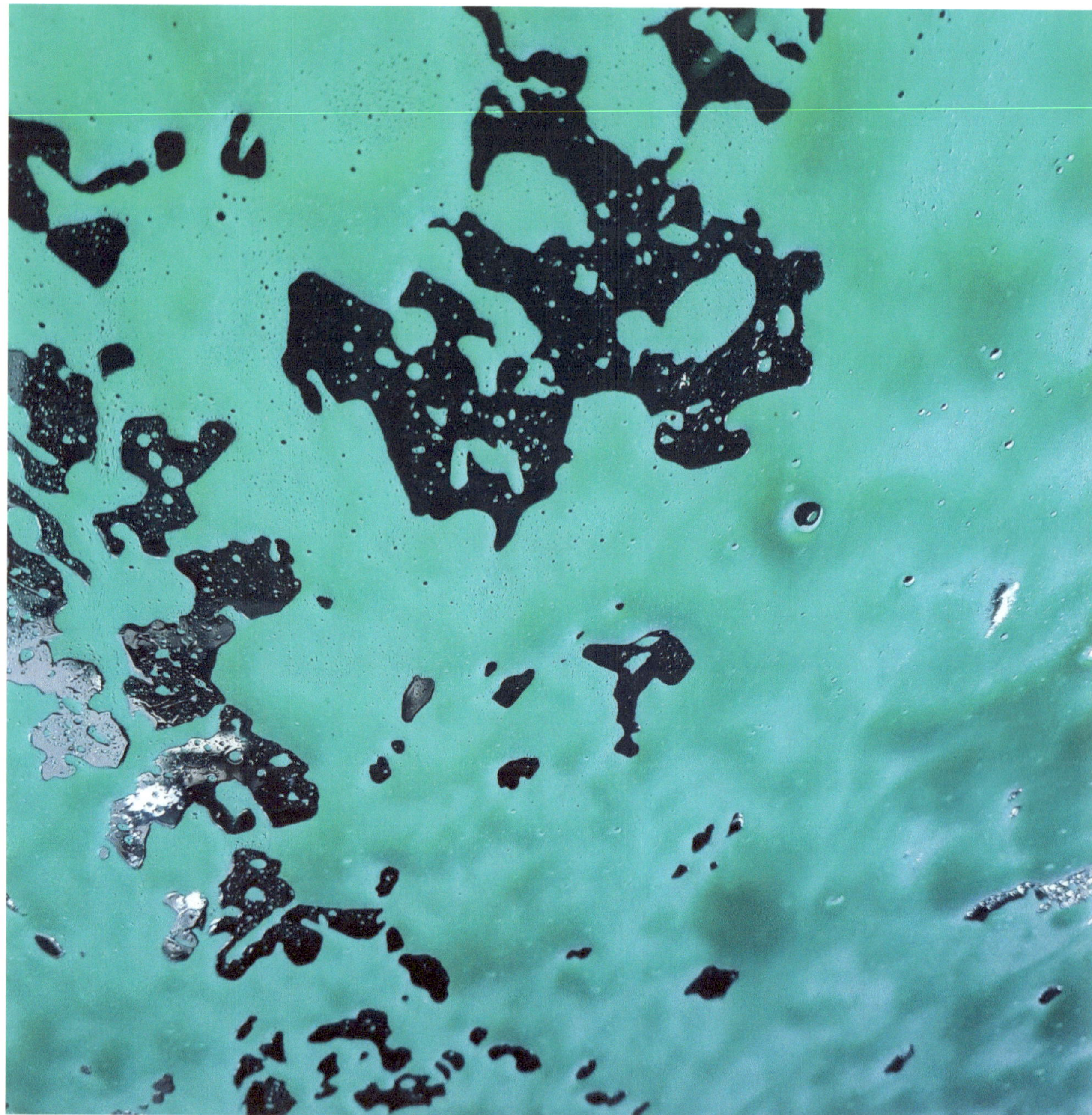

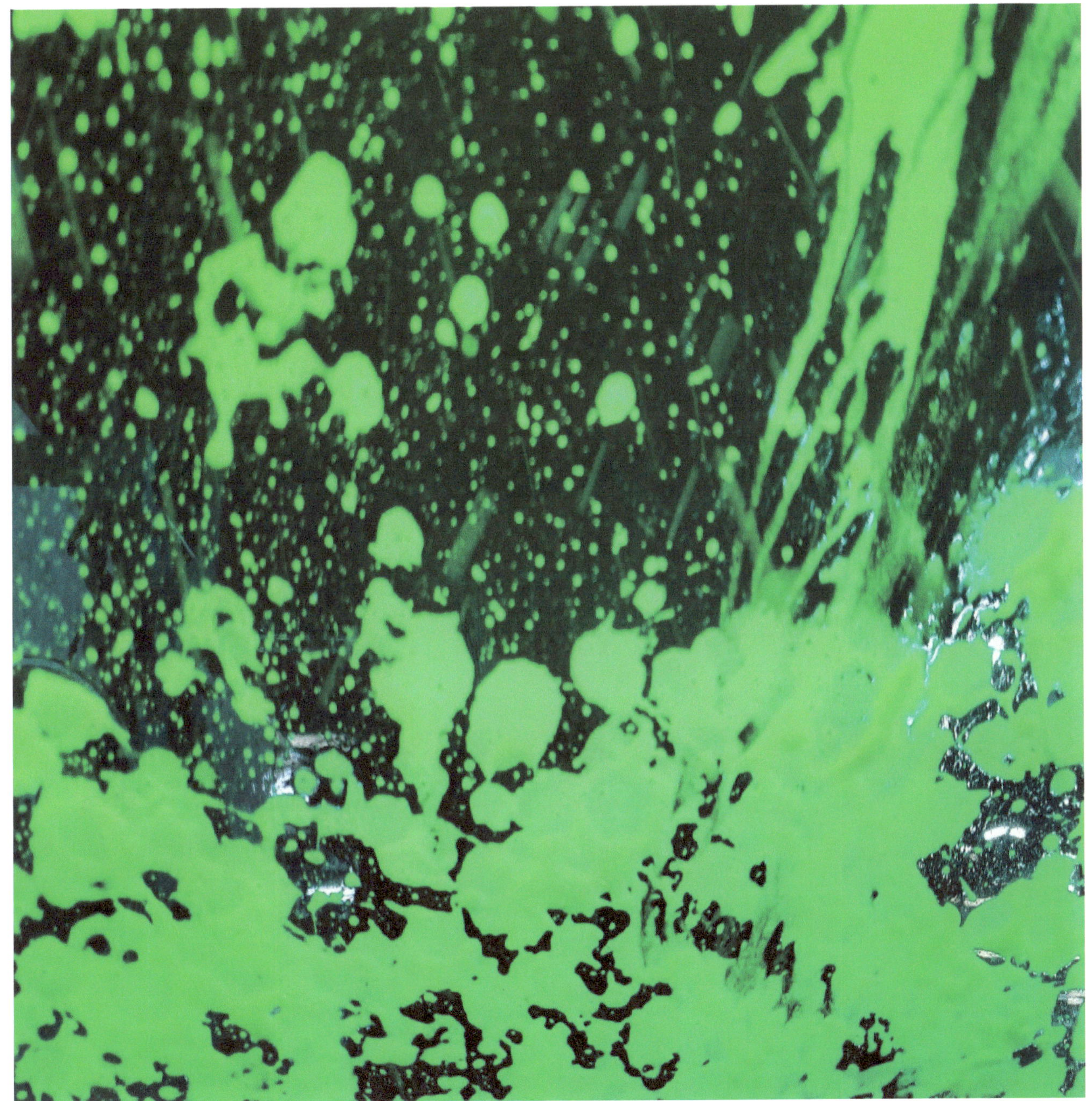

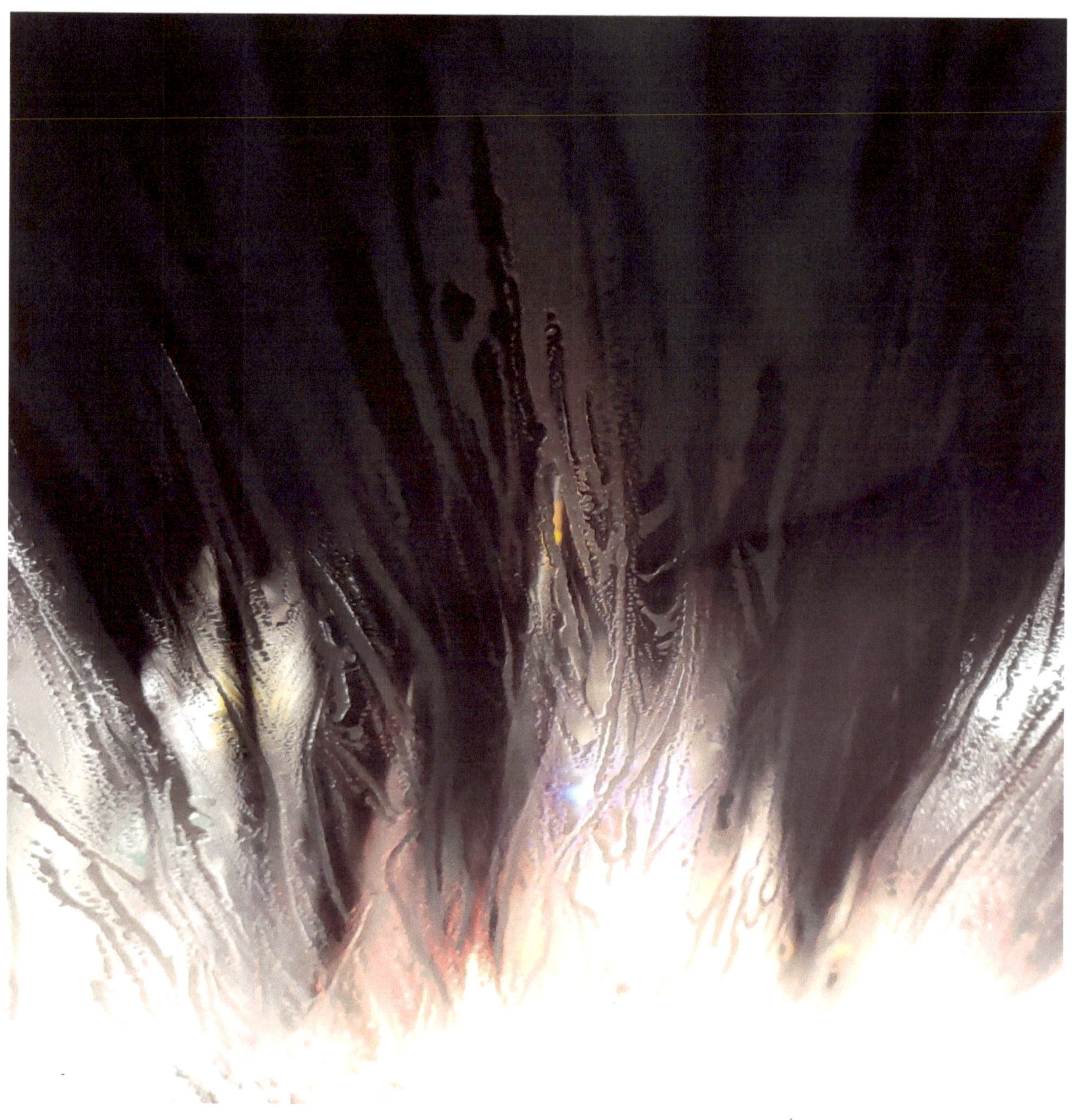

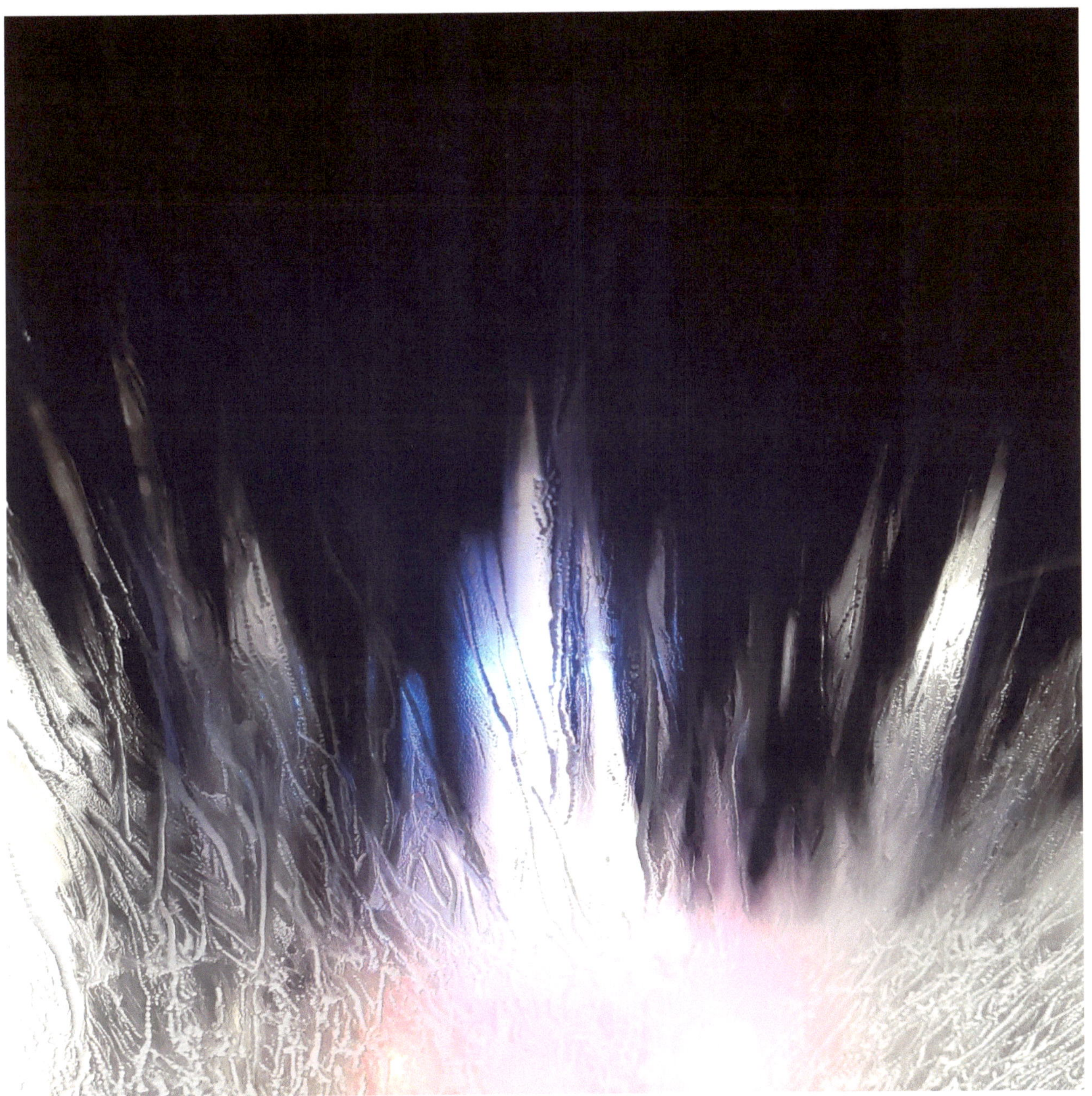

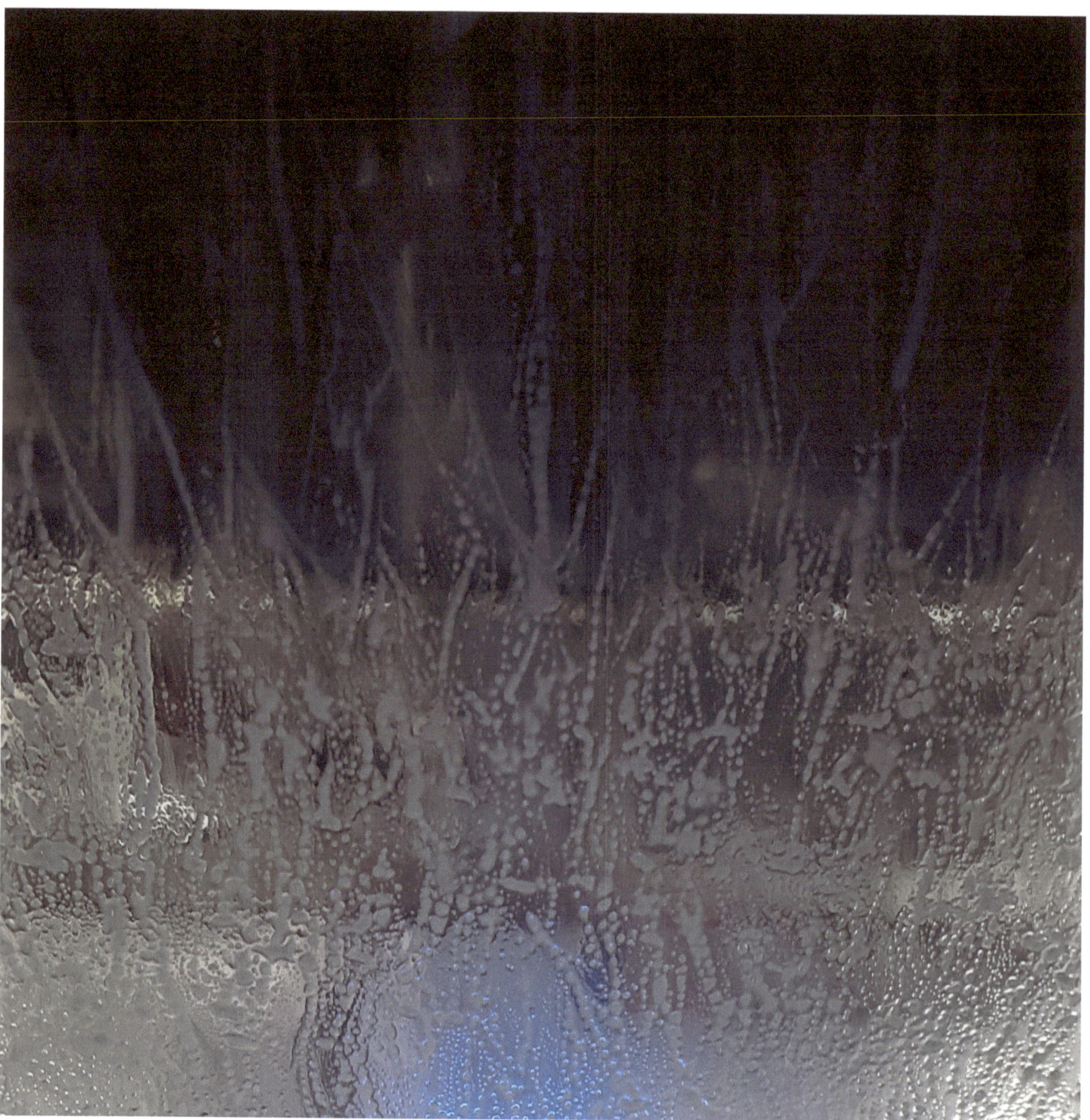

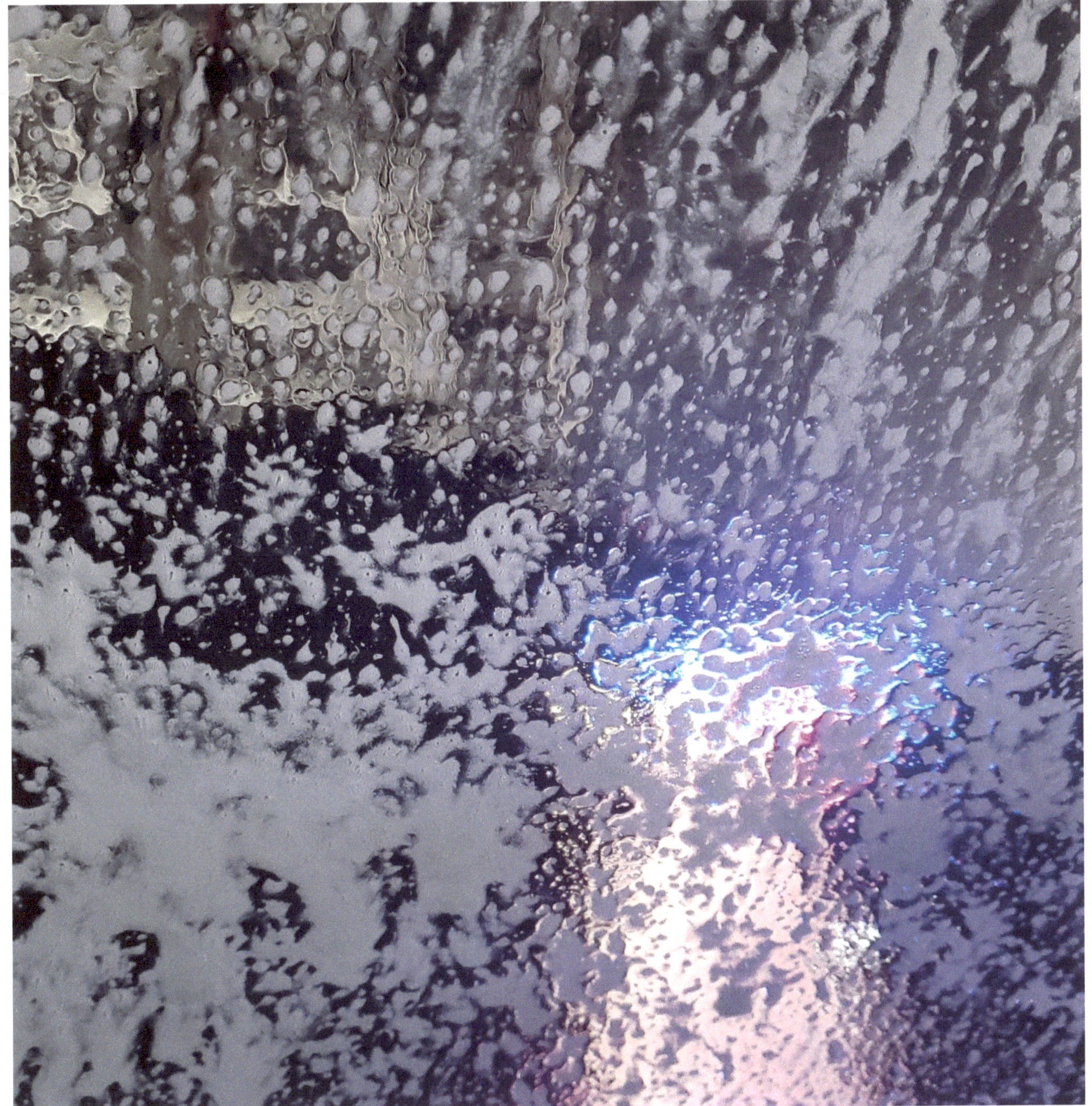

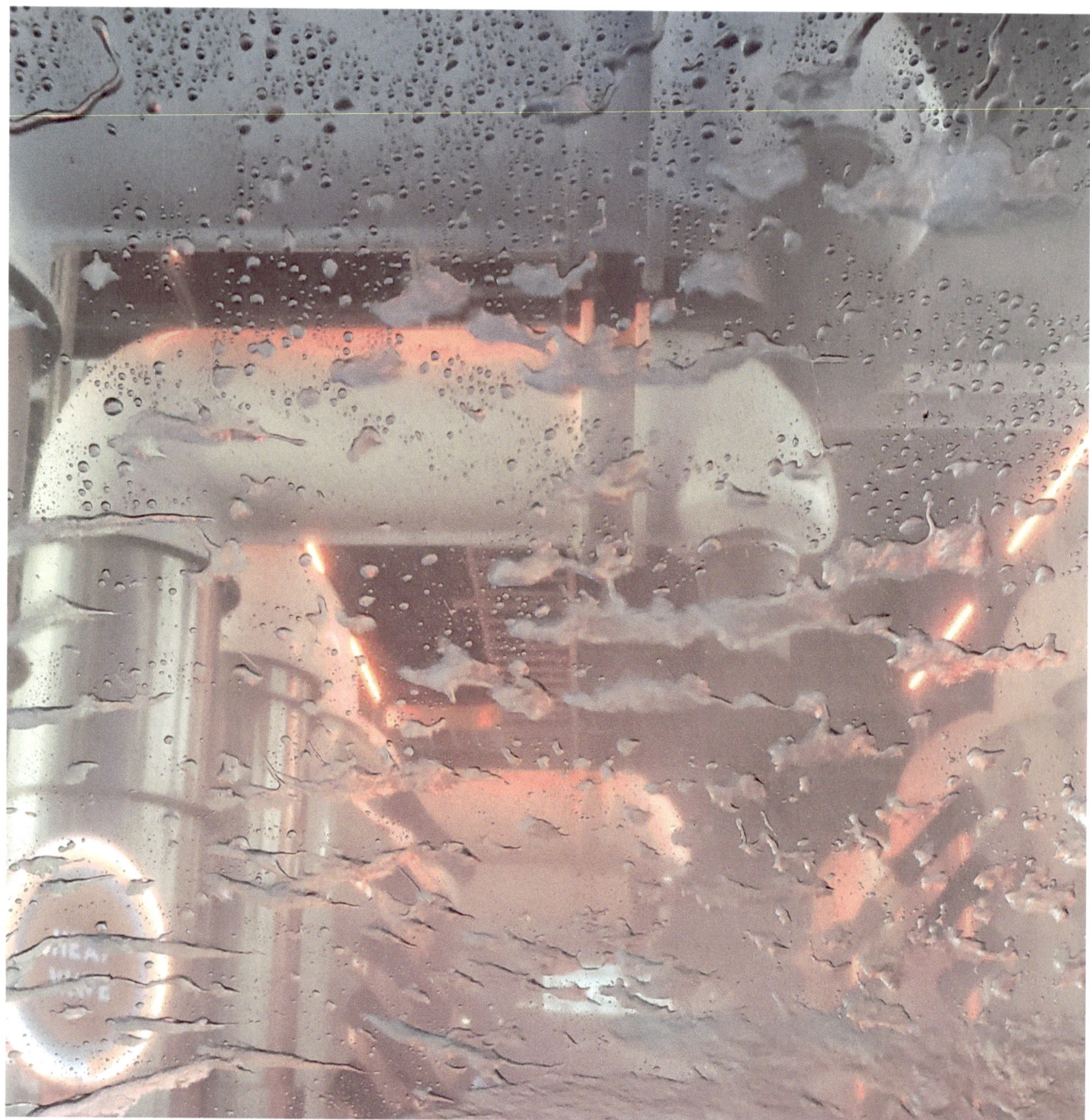

www.ingramcontent.com/pod-product-compliance
Lightning Source LLC
Chambersburg PA
CBHW042050100726
47973CB00014B/203

9798218191474